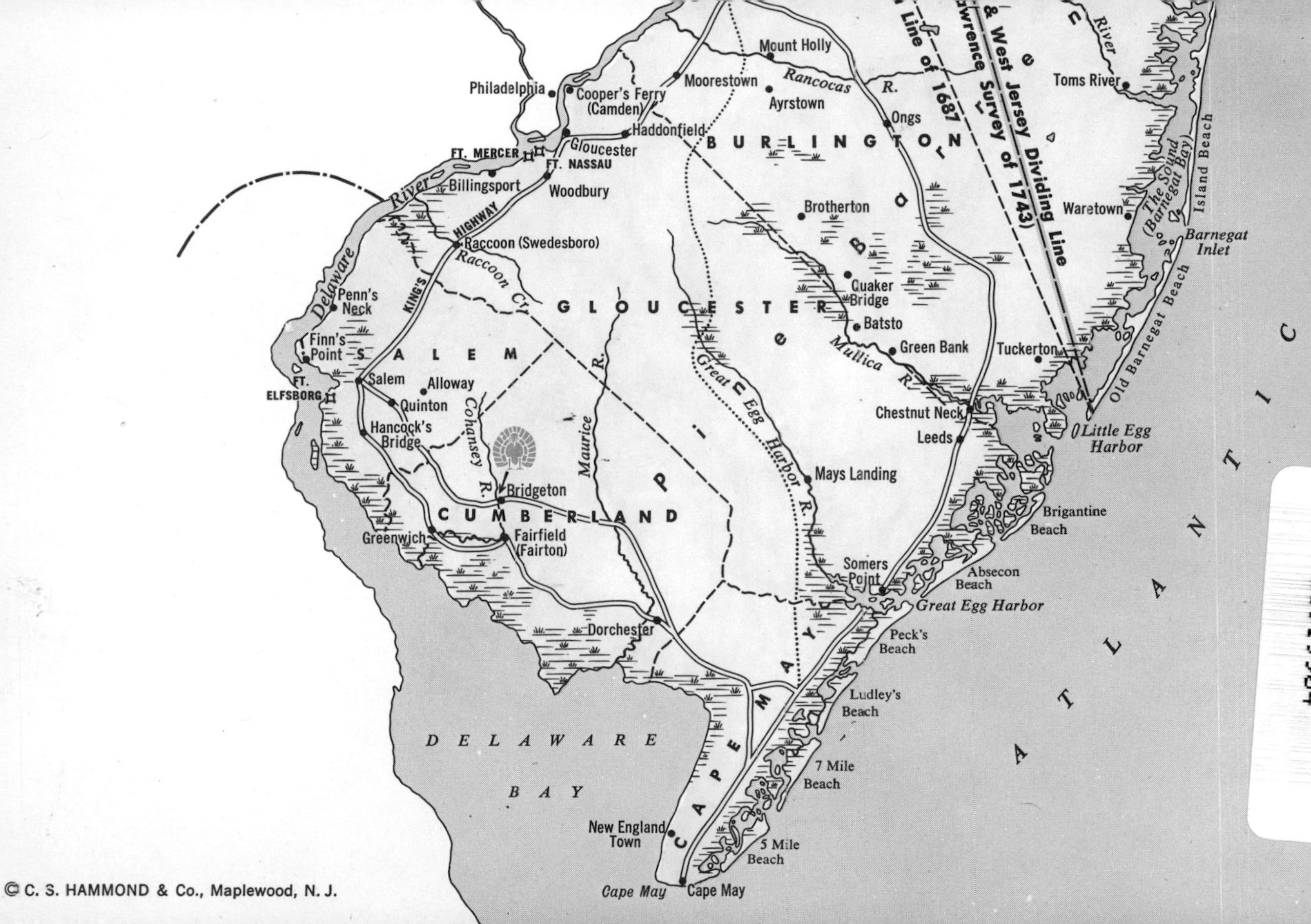

& West Jersey Dividing Line
awrence Survey of 1743)
Line of 1687
BURLINGTON
GLOUCESTER
SALEM
CUMBERLAND
CAPE MAY
Philadelphia
Cooper's Ferry (Camden)
Haddonfield
Moorestown
Mount Holly
Rancocas R.
Ayrstown
Ongs
Toms River
River
Waretown
The Sound (Barnegat Bay)
Island Beach
Barnegat Inlet
Old Barnegat Beach
Little Egg Harbor
Tuckerton
Brotherton
Quaker Bridge
Batsto
Green Bank
Mullica R.
Chestnut Neck
Leeds
Brigantine Beach
Absecon Beach
Great Egg Harbor
Somers Point
Mays Landing
Great Egg Harbor R.
Peck's Beach
Ludley's Beach
7 Mile Beach
5 Mile Beach
Cape May
New England Town
Dorchester
DELAWARE BAY
Fairfield (Fairton)
Greenwich
Bridgeton
Cohansey R.
Maurice R.
Hancock's Bridge
Quinton
Alloway
Salem
FT. ELFSBORG
Finn's Point
Penn's Neck
Delaware River
KING'S HIGHWAY
Raccoon (Swedesboro)
Raccoon Cr.
Billingsport
Woodbury
FT. MERCER
FT. NASSAU
Gloucester
ATLANTIC OCE

Elementary Education in New Jersey: A History

THE NEW JERSEY HISTORICAL SERIES

Edited by

RICHARD M. HUBER   WHEATON J. LANE

New Jersey from Colony to State—1609-1789	Richard P. McCormick
New Jersey and the Civil War	Earl Schenck Miers
New Jersey and the English Colonization of North America	Wesley Frank Craven
The Story of the Jersey Shore	Harold F. Wilson
Princeton and Rutgers—The Two Colonial Colleges of New Jersey	George P. Schmidt
Architecture in New Jersey	Alan Gowans
Elementary Education in New Jersey: A History	Roscoe L. West
The New Jersey High School: A History	Robert D. Bole and Laurence B. Johnson
The New Jersey Proprietors and Their Lands	John E. Pomfret
The Early Dutch and Swedish Settlers of New Jersey	Adrian C. Leiby
New Jersey and the American Revolution	Alfred Hoyt Bill
Radicals and Visionaries: A History of Dissent in New Jersey	Morris Schonbach
Religion in New Jersey	Wallace N. Jamison
The New Jersey Governor: A Study in Political Power	Duane Lockard
The Research State: A History of Science in New Jersey	John R. Pierce and Arthur G. Tressler

Other books in the series will be announced

Volume 7

The New Jersey Historical Series

Elementary Education in New Jersey: A History

ROSCOE L. WEST

1964

D. VAN NOSTRAND COMPANY, INC.

Princeton, New Jersey

New York, N. Y. • Toronto, Canada • London, England

D. VAN NOSTRAND COMPANY, INC.
120 Alexander St., Princeton, New Jersey (*Principal office*)
24 West 40 Street, New York 18, New York

D. VAN NOSTRAND COMPANY, LTD.
358, Kensington High Street, London, W.14, England

D. VAN NOSTRAND COMPANY (*Canada*), LTD.
25 Hollinger Road, Toronto 16, Canada

Published simultaneously in Canada by
D. VAN NOSTRAND COMPANY (Canada), LTD.

PRINTED IN THE UNITED STATES OF AMERICA

FOREWORD

Many tracks will be left by the New Jersey Tercentenary celebration, but few will be larger than those made by the New Jersey Historical Series. The Series is a monumental publishing project—the product of a remarkable collaborative effort between public and private enterprise.

New Jersey has needed a series of books about itself. The 300th anniversary of the State is a fitting time to publish such a series. It is to the credit of the State's Tercentenary Commission that this series has been created.

In an enterprise of such scope, there must be many contributors. Each of these must give considerably of himself if the enterprise is to succeed. The New Jersey Historical Series, the most ambitious publishing venture ever undertaken about a state, was conceived by a committee of Jerseymen—Julian P. Boyd, Wesley Frank Craven, John T. Cunningham, David S. Davies, and Richard P. McCormick. Not only did these men outline the need for such an historic venture; they also aided in the selection of the editors of the series.

Both jobs were well done. The volumes speak for themselves. The devoted and scholarly services of

Richard M. Huber and Wheaton J. Lane, the editors, are a part of every book in the series. The editors have been aided in their work by two fine assistants, Elizabeth Jackson Holland and Bertha DeGraw Miller.

To D. Van Nostrand Company, Inc. my special thanks for recognizing New Jersey's need and for bringing their skills and publishing wisdom to bear upon the printing and distributing of the New Jersey Historical Series.

My final and most heartfelt thanks must go to Roscoe L. West, who accepted my invitation to write *Elementary Education in New Jersey: A History,* doing so at great personal sacrifice and without thought of material gain. We are richer by his scholarship. We welcome this important contribution to an understanding of our State.

RICHARD J. HUGHES
Governor of the
State of New Jersey

January, 1964

PREFACE

The public school system, providing opportunities for all children, is accepted as a necessary element of our society. Most people take for granted the excellent facilities of modern school buildings and the high standard of education required of teachers. They are not aware of the long struggle which took place to establish the common public school and to bring it to its present state. The campaign came from the "grass roots." It was not a movement of educators but came from the common folk who demanded that their governent make the schools the keystone of democracy.

In this book the author has tried to show how the development of the democratic concept of equality of opportunity has been interwoven with the growth of the public school for all of the children. In the nineteenth century, people were fighting for common public education as the chief means of giving their children the power to advance in a democratic society which was developing in the New World. In the early twentieth century the public school was of tremendous importance in giving to the new immigrants the knowledge and skills required for adapting themselves to their adopted country. To-day the schools are in the forefront in the struggle of racial groups for realization of equality of opportunity.

Much attention has been given to the education of teachers because of the author's belief that the teacher is the most important factor in the entire school program. The efficiency of the educational process depends very largely on the quality of the teacher. Changing patterns of education can be successful only as teachers are equipped to meet new requirements.

I am particularly indebted to Miss Doris Perry, Reference Librarian, Trenton State College for assistance in connection with early materials. Professor Dorothy G. Petersen of the Trenton State College and Miss Anne S. Hoppock, Director, Elementary State Department of Education were extremely helpful in their suggestions concerning our present-day schools. Dr. S. David Winans, Director, Bureau of Research, State Department of Education guided me to the valuable reports and documents of that department. In connection with illustrations I am indebted to Mrs. James M. Ralston of the "Colonial Dames," to Dr. Cleve O. Westby, Director, School Building Services, State Department of Education, to Miss Anita Kreuger of Irvington, and to the publicity staff of the New Jersey Education Association. The editors of the Tercentenary Series, Richard M. Huber and Wheaton J. Lane gave me very valuable criticisms and suggestions.

Trenton, New Jersey
January, 1964

ROSCOE L. WEST

TABLE OF CONTENTS

LIST OF ILLUSTRATIONS

Courtesy of H. Armstrong Roberts

I

COLONIAL DIVERSITIES

THE PEOPLE WHO SETTLED New Jersey came from several countries in Europe. They spoke different languages and belonged to a variety of religious sects. There was, therefore, a greater diversity of background than in most other colonies, especially those in New England. Prior to 1664 when the English took over from the Dutch, Hollanders from New Amsterdam had settled the northern section, principally along the Hudson river. Swedes moved into the southwestern part of the colony. After 1664, Englishmen and Scots came in increasing numbers along with settlers from New England; later, Germans made their appearance. In 1702, when the provinces of East Jersey and West Jersey were united, it is estimated that from these various sources there were about fifteen thousand people in the colony.

The lack of homogeneity was an important factor in the development of education. It prevented New Jersey from taking definite steps towards community responsibility for education. The first education laws of the New Jersey colony were passed in 1693 and 1695 by the General Assembly of East Jersey. These, briefly, provided that the inhabitants of a town could meet, select three representatives who were authorized to hire a teacher, and fix rates to be paid by the inhabitants of the town for their children who attended school. It was nearly two hundred years later when a system of public education for all children supported by taxation was approved. New Jersey was considerably behind the New England states in taking this step.

Education in the seventeenth century was considered the responsibility of the home and church. To understand the nature of education at that time, it is necessary to examine the ideas current in the various countries from which the settlers came, as well as the practices of the different religious groups in providing for the education of their children.

These influences produced developments quite different from those in New England where the early settlers were largely from one group. Massachusetts, for example, under the influence of the English Puritans took important steps in 1642 and again in 1647 toward establishing the concept of community responsibility for education. Her famous Law of 1642 placed upon the town officials the duty of ascertaining whether the children were being taught "to read and understand the principles of religion and the capital laws of the country." This is a remarkable law. For the first time in the English-speaking world, a legislative body was ordering that all children be taught to read. The concept arose out of a Reformation conviction that the individual was responsible for his own salvation. Thus the masses must be able to read the Bible themselves in the vernacular, and it was the duty of the government to see that this was possible.

Actually the Law of 1642 did not establish schools nor did it direct the employment of schoolmasters. The citizens were still responsible. Soon, the people began to see that more than this was necessary. In 1647 another law was passed. In the preamble was the warning that "one chief point of that old deluder, Satan, is to keep men from a knowledge of the Scriptures . . . . by keeping them in an unknown tongue," so that now "by persuading from the use of tongues" learning was in danger "of being buried in the grave of our fathers in church and commonwealth." The law provided:

That every town having fifty householders should at once

appoint a teacher of reading and writing and provide for his wages in such a manner as the town might determine; and *That* every town having a hundred householders must provide a (Latin) grammar school to fit the youths for the university under penalty of £5 for failure to do so.

Thus it was ordered that a school system be started. These laws embodied three important concepts: that universal education is essential to the well-being of the state, the obligation for education rests primarily with the parents, and that the state can enforce this obligation and raise money for this purpose through a general tax.

Massachusetts represented one approach: the "compulsory maintenance" attitude. The state was serving the church. It passed laws compelling the provision of educational facilities, thus establishing a tradition of management and support which lasted even after the state and church had parted company.

New Jersey and Pennsylvania developed the "parochial school" attitude. The early settlers in New Jersey were Protestant in faith, but from a variety of national backgrounds and religious denominations. As no one sect was in a majority, it seemed best to allow each group to control its own schools. Although the laws reflected the belief that it was desirable for the common people to read and understand the Bible, they also indicated a belief that each church should educate its children according to its own methods. Education, therefore, did not appeal to the central government for aid but depended on the initiative of the various churches. Consequently, schools would thrive in enterprising church centers and lapse in places where the church was weak. Settlements were often far apart. Many were seriously hampered by the primary necessity of getting enough to eat. Communication was difficult, so it is easy to understand that each community was dependent on its own resources and efforts.

The Dutch who settled along the Hudson brought with them traditions of education which combined control by both state and church. Even in the sixteenth century elementary education in Holland was widespread and most peasants could read. The state legally owned and controlled the schools, but the church generally appointed the teachers. Fees were paid, but the towns also contributed. Schoolmasters in Holland usually had other duties in the church such as choirmaster or sexton, and we find this practice carried to the new country. Naturally religion and morals were stressed, and the curriculum was pretty well limited to reading and writing and a little arithmetic.

The first elementary school in the New Jersey settlements along the Hudson seems to have been that at Bergen in 1662. The first schoolmaster, Englebert Steenhuysen, was paid a salary and certain amounts from fees collected from the parents. It is recorded that, when he was asked to contribute to the maintenance of a soldier, he resigned, claiming that the schoolmaster should be exempt from village taxes.

Bergen tried somewhat later to maintain a free school and ran into difficulties because the people in the outlying regions objected to being taxed. These people appealed to the governor, but were ordered to pay. Similar schools sprang up as Dutch settlements arose in other parts of the colony. As the Dutch reached the Raritan Valley, many local churches established schools. They had considerable vitality in the eighteenth century, but their popularity declined as the demand for public education grew. Parochial schools went out of favor and the desire for education among the later descendants of the first Dutch settlers showed itself in a campaign for public education.

The Swedes brought with them rich educational traditions. The Reformation had broadened an interest in education which had been developing since the Middle Ages. But the Swedish settlements in New Jersey were few and far between, and the struggle for existence was hard. Ministers of the Lutheran Church tried to teach children the Catechism and some reading and writing. There was no money for schoolmasters as such and, after the English took over in 1664, no more funds came from the old country in Europe. The Revolution dealt a serious blow to the parochial schools. By the end of the eighteenth century very little was left of Swedish culture. Unable to survive as a distinct group they tended to unite with those who, in the first half of the nineteenth century, carried their religious zeal into the movement for free, public schools.

For two centuries Quakers were very influential in the political and educational affairs of New Jersey. The Quakers were always motivated by three basic ideals: piety, practicality, and philanthropy. They did not require higher education for a ministry, but depended on what they called "the inner light." Yet leaders like George Fox and George Keith did much to encourage education for children. For many years, Quakers were the most numerous of the religious groups in central and southern New Jersey. Their yearly, monthly, and quarterly meetings knit them into a well-functioning unit, and reports show how much attention they paid to schools and to moral and religious instruction. They believed firmly in manual work and devoted much time to the problems of apprenticeship and to the placement of poor and orphan children in families that would attend to their education.

In 1682, the West Jersey Assembly granted Matinicunck Island, a three-hundred-acre tract, to Burlington for the maintenance of a school. For over one hundred years no income from the island was secured, or sought because of doubts as to the legality of the title. But, in 1767, under the influence of the Quakers, the town voted to use revenues obtained from the island to help teach poor children. In the early part of the nineteenth century these proceeds were used by the town to help support all schools and thus reduce fees charged to the parents. Later in the century land for schools was purchased from this fund, and part of the amount necessary for the erection of seven school buildings also came from this source. The island is now called "Burlington Island" and the income from its land is still used for public education. At present the revenue is approximately fifteen hundred dollars per year and the money is used for instructional materials which would be difficult to secure from the regular budget. It is interesting that a separate Board of Managers has always existed for the control of funds derived from the island. Every year, the citizens of Burlington are called to a "Town Meeting" to elect managers and to approve of their actions.

Two famous Quaker proponents of education were Anthony Benezet and John Woolman. The latter was an ardent believer in freeing the Negroes from slavery and carried his liberal ideas into education. He was born in Rancocas in 1720 and devoted his life to humane and progressive causes. In a monthly meeting of Friends held in Burlington in 1774, the following is part of a Testimony given for him:

> He several times opened a school at Mount Holly for the instruction of poor Friends' children and others, being concerned for their help and improvement therein. His love and care for the rising youth among us was truly great.

Anthony Benezet did away with brutal punishments. He was also a noted author of textbooks. To him children were children and not miniature adults.

For well over a hundred years the Quakers conducted successful schools, from Plainfield and Rahway in the center of the state to Little Egg Harbor and Salem in the south. Other influential centers were located in Shrewsbury, Moorestown, Burlington, and Mount Holly, and there were Quaker schools in several other communities. In 1831 and again in 1838, new laws made it possible for church groups requiring education as a part of their discipline to receive State money. This benefitted the Quakers who were fearful that decline of their schools would subject their children to evil, secular influences. But having once received State funds and become somewhat dependent on them, many of the schools closed after the repeal, in 1866, of the law granting money to church schools. They then joined in the campaign for public and common education.

The Quaker schools rendered substantial services before public schools were established. They set standards which undoubtedly strengthened the efforts of those who believed in an efficient system of education for all of the children of all of the people.

Among the other groups in the colony and in New Jersey in the eighteenth and nineteenth centuries, the Germans of the Moravian and the Lutheran Churches had some influence. Several groups of settlers came from Philadelphia into southern New Jersey, and others to the upper part of the Delaware and the banks of the Raritan. Education was very closely associated with the churches, and its quality varied with the pastors. The stronger groups, in Philadelphia and New York were also of considerable influence.

In the second half of the seventeenth century there was a rebirth of piety and religion in Germany, and this was communicated to the settlers in the new country. Theerfore, there was great emphasis on the Catechism and, sometimes, on preserving the German language and culture. In the colonial period, the German groups can be credited with the promotion of a conservative, religious education for the children of their own parishes. Theirs was a parochial approach without any apparent understanding of the responsibiilty of the entire community to educate all of the children.

The Church of England had few adherents in New Jersey at the end of the seventeenth century. The officials who came from England, after the Proprietors handed over their rights of government to Queen Anne in 1702, were not particularly interested in the education of children. When Lord Cornbury was appointed governor in 1702, he was given a list of 103 Articles to guide him in administering the affairs of the colony. These go into great detail concerning matters of government, trade policies, relations with the mother country, and so on.

There are even six articles providing counsel on the promotion of religious exercises, the approval of ministers by the Bishop of London, and other such matters, but there is not one article concerning education, even for the encouragement of teaching under the auspices of the Church. In fact, the governing group in England showed its fear of education and the dissemination of ideas in the following article:

> Forasmuch as great inconveniences may arise by the liberty of printing in our said province, you are to provide for all necessary orders, that no person keep any press for printing, nor that any book, pamphlet or other matters whatsoever be printed without your especial leave and license obtained.

In 1701, there had been formed the famous Society for the Propagation of the Gospel in Foreign Parts. This group did outstanding work in organizing parish schools. A missionary named John Talbot traveled through the colony promoting the establishment of new parishes and trying to establish new schools. Naturally the chief object of these schools was to teach the Catechism; but reading, writing, and arithmetic were also included. By 1712 he had succeeded in getting a schoolhouse erected in Burlington, but parents did not send their children regularly when they were needed on the farm or for other work, and they did not pay their fees with promptness. A few other schools were somewhat more prosperous, but then the Revolution intervened. Many of the parishes were interested, however, in the free education for Negroes, and, in a way, this laid the foundation for the public common schools.

George Doane, who was elected bishop of New Jersey in 1832, believed in general education but came to fear that the secular influence of the public schools would be detrimental to the religious development of children. He desired church schools which would form a complete Episcopal system of education. In 1837 he was instrumental in the founding of St. Mary's Hall for girls in

Burlington which still does outstanding work in elementary as well as secondary education. Even some of the friends of Bishop Doane, such as Judge Richard S. Field of Princeton, who was instrumental in the fight for the common school and for the normal school, could not share his zeal for the parochial school. Indeed, after 1860 the Episcopal schools began to decline rapidly, especially in the elementary field. They made great contributions at a time when the community in general was not prepared to take over the responsibility for general common school education, but they gave way before the spread of public elementary schools.

Following the Restoration of the monarchy in England in 1660 with the accession of Charles II, the Presbyterians who had been powerful during the years under Cromwell were persecuted and began to look to the new country for settlement. Scots and North Irishmen soon came to New Jersey and scattered through of the colony. Naturally they brought with them their religious and educational ideals. Under the influence of Calvin and Knox they believed in individual responsibility for salvation and therefore advocated general education sufficient to reading the Bible and adhering to the pronouncements of the church. Many of the leaders desired a system of education which would extend through the university level.

As the eighteenth century progressed, many parochial schools were attached to the churches. By the nineteenth century the leaders were urging more attention to parochial education because they feared that religious training was impossible in common schools. Presbyterians debated at length whether to work harder for their own schools or to join in the growing movement for the public common school. Again, the leaders favored the parochial idea, but the individual churches were not in accord. Some did not care for centralized control, some feared high costs, and many felt that the public common school was necessary in a developing democracy. The successful parochial schools provided for good teachers, proper supervision, and adequate textbooks. The course of study was based on religion, but included writing, arithmetic, elementary geography, general science, and some singing which, of course, was mainly religious. After the advance in the laws providing for the common school in the middle of the nineteenth century, the Presbyterian schools declined rapidly and finally lost significance on the elementary level of education.

The efforts of both the Baptists and Methodists in the educational field were mainly on the secondary and higher levels. Neither group made any distinctive contribution on the elementary level, although in 1779 John Honeywell of Knowlton bequeathed to the Philadelphia Association a fund to establish a school for slaves and poor children. A schoolhouse was built for this purpose near Hope in Warren County.

There were few Roman Catholics in the colony in the early days. Such prejudice existed that no educational activity was possible before the middle of the nineteenth century. In whatever parts Jews settled, they fostered education, but there were very few in New Jersey before the middle of the nineteenth century. In general they established their own schools for religious instruction, but depended on the public schools for secular learning. Some of their leaders were prominent in the campaigns for the public common school.

Most classes in the colonial period were held in churches or in rooms connected with them. Some schoolhouses were built by groups or even by individuals. Often they were ill adapted to school use: poorly heated and equipped with makeshift furniture. One notable exception was the "Old School House" which still stands in Mount Holly. It was built in 1759, when 21 citizens of Mount Holly or Bridgetown (nine Quakers, eight Episcopalians, and four whose religion is unknown) subscribed 25 shares to buy land and build a schoolhouse. They bought a small lot on the north side of New Street (now Brainerd Street). The schoolhouse was brick and had a large fireplace. It was restored by the National Society of

Colonial Dames of America in 1959 and has been since refurnished as it was originally. There is some evidence that John Woolman taught in this schoolhouse. Classes were held in this building for over fifty years. Terms were irregular, and the schoolmaster was paid by the parents. In 1815 the heirs of the original builders deeded the old schoolhouse to the Female Benevolent Society which proposed to teach gratis "in a public School" all the poor children of Mount Holly and its vicinity. During the next 33 years, over a thousand children were taught without charge in the "Free School House," as it was then called.

In summary, it can be said that for over one hundred and fifty years the education of children of elementary school age in New Jersey was conducted under the auspices of the various religious sects represented in the population. Each group wished to assure itself that the religious and moral standards of its own particular sect would be passed on to the children of its communicants.

From the Dutch came a democratic tradition in educational policy. They established elementary schools at an early date, common to all and supported by all. The English educational policy was essentially an aristocratic system in nature. Parents were expected to pay for the education of their children, and public support was given only to the poor. The Scots and Scotch-Irish believed in universal education but for many years encouraged only schools under the control of the churches. The Quakers declared in their church "discipline" for the education of children, but for a long time were an obstacle to public education in general because of their separateness. The settlers from New England brought with them the ideas of the Puritans for general common education supported by all.

The religious groups did little for the education of teachers, depending on part-time employees of the churches and others devoted to religious education. Little progress was made in the expansion of the curriculum beyond religious instruction, reading, spelling, writing,

The Old School House in Mount Holly as restored by the National Society of Colonial Dames of America in 1959. This building was erected by citizens of Mount Holly in 1759, and was far superior to most schoolhouses of that time.

and simple arithmetic. They made no efforts to cooperate in securing common school education until the population increased, became more varied, and began to be infused with democratic ideas after the Revolution.

Religious diversity in the colony undoubtedly led to a lack of unity among the people for the advancement of common school education. Church people feared the supposed secular influences of the public school and therefore were reluctant to surrender the advantages which they felt accrued from the school operated by the church.

On the other hand, their activities were undoubtedly of great value in educating many children of elementary

Interior of the Old School House in Mount Holly as restored, showing the type of desk originally used and the fireplace which heated the school.

school age before the people as a whole were ready for the free school supported from public funds. They advocated education of the poor and of the Negroes and thus, in a way, prepared the position of those who advocated public education of all children. As time went on, religious motives led many church leaders to campaign for free public education as a right of all children and as a foundation of democratic government.

II

COMMON SCHOOL BEGINNINGS

FROM THE TIME of the appointment of English governors, in 1702, until the Revolution, no significant advances in education for children of elementary school age were made. Then the Revolution prevented any immediate changes; so it was not until the end of the eighteenth century that there were stirrings toward a more efficient system of public education. During this century only two kinds of schools were in operation in addition to those maintained by the religious groups: free schools for the children of the poor, and schools opened to the public on a subscription basis. The Society for the Propagation of the Gospel did much to promote the English "charity-school" and devised rules and regulations for the employment of schoolmasters who demonstrated good character, conformity to the doctrine of the Church of England, and ability to teach reading, writing, and the Catechism. Their activities produced jealousy among other sects but did much to further the idea of democratic education.

The schools for children whose parents could pay the fees charged were often in homes and sometimes a college graduate, often from New England, could be found as a teacher. "Dame schools" also were opened, usually held in the home of the teacher. The "Dame school" was brought to New England from England where the name had denoted a school taught by a matron in her home while she also attended to her household duties.

The first seventy-five years of the nineteenth century constituted an era of relentless campaigning for free public education and for better preparation of teachers. The two campaigns went forward together, and men who were champions of one also worked hard for the other. They realized that the two were interrelated and that without good teachers there could be no permanent improvement in the public school system. Following the Revolution and the establishment of the new government, many people began to see that a democratic form of government could not function well without the education of those who had the power of the ballot. Leaders of the Republic expressed themselves forcibly in favor of education for citizenship.

The famous Northwest Ordinance of 1787 contained the following statement: "Religion, morality and knowledge being necessary to good government and the happiness of mankind, schools and the means of education shall forever be encouraged."

Washington had said in his Farewell Address:

> Promote, then, as an object of primary importance, institutions for the general diffusion of knowledge. In proportion as the structure of a government gives force to public opinion, it is essential that public opinion be enlightened.

Jefferson expressed his ideas on education in his "Notes on the State of Virginia," an edition of which was published in Trenton in 1803. He had been instrumental in writing new laws for Virginia to promote the common school. Madison had expressed himself to the effect that, "Knowledge will govern ignorance; and a people who mean to be their own governors must arm themselves with the power which knowledge gives."

"The emerging power of the common man" was in the air. Men believed that knowledge would produce virtue and that crime would disappear if men were educated. History has dispelled this naïve assumption. We realize today that education is a means to be used for good or ill by the persons who receive it. It contains no talisman for the sudden reformation of individuals or of society. This nineteenth-century faith in education as a salvation for individuals and for the group was a powerful motive in the fight for widening and bettering educational opportunity. Perhaps, in our present faith in the opportunities which education gives, we have merely rephrased in a little more practical way the simple faith which fired the pioneers of the early nineteenth century. To many of them education for all was a spiritual fulfillment of the rights of the common man for which they and their fathers had fought.

Many began to see that a new society could not be formed without a fresh conception of education and its relationship to economic and social opportunities. A dream emerged—a dream of a common school supported by public funds, in which children of the rich and the poor and of all creeds and national backgrounds would learn together. Through this agency would come a new kind of person, an "American," dedicated to the ideals on which the Republic was founded, the ideals expressed in the Declaration of Independence and the Constitution. Leaders began to think of the common school as a means of realizing the principles for which the Revolution was fought and as an agency for teaching newcomers the ways of a new democratic life.

A leader who caught fire from the statements of nationally important men, particularly from Jefferson, was James Parker of Perth Amboy. Although a Federalist, he fought with the opposite party for the rights of the common schools. For years he battled in the Assembly for State aid to the townships. Finally, in 1817, the Legislature established the State School Fund, allocating some United States bonds and graually adding other stock and appropriations. This was really the first step taken towards the establishment of a public common school system. In 1818 another law appointed the governor and certain other State officials as Trustees of this Fund and required an annual report. The fund grew although no appropriations to the townships were actually made until 1829. At that time the fund amounted to two hundred and forty-five thousand dollars, and twenty thousand dollars was appropriated to aid the poorer districts.

In 1820, after much agitation, another law was passed authorizing townships to raise money for school purposes but still only for those conisdered too poor to pay the rates charged, as shown from the following excerpt from the law:

> That hereafter, it shall be lawful for the inhabitants in each of the townships in this State, duly qualified to vote, at town meetings . . . at their annual meetings to vote, grant and raise . . . moneys for town purposes. . . . Such sum of money to be laid out and expended for the education of such poor children as are paupers, . . . and the children of such poor parents resident in said townships, as are . . . unable to pay for schooling the same.

Meanwhile, many people were beginning to talk about the number of children in the State who were receiving little or no education, and a movement was initiated in favor of legislation which would provide a system of public schools. A group calling itself the "Friends of Education" distributed pamphlets throughout New Jersey and appointed Robert Baird, a minister, to visit those parts of the State destitute of educational advantages, to help establish schools, secure teachers, and organize the people in favor of better laws for education. Many meetings were held and facts about the deplorable conditions of the schools secured. John Maclean, then Professor of Mathematics at the College of New Jersey which was to become Princeton University, and later its President, advocated many of the features of the educational system which we have today, including a state board of education, a state superintendent, and certification of teachers. In 1827, James Parker,, again a member of the Legislature, advocated support of the common schools and establishment of a normal school. Finally, in 1829 an "Act to Establish Common Schools" was passed. Among other things, it provided for appropriations from the State School Fund, for election of a school committee of three in each township, for licensing of teachers, provisions of schoolhouses, and proper reports to the State.

The proponents of this act had presented a number of arguments: that free public schools would prevent class differentiation, that church and private schools had proved inadequate, that a system of religious schools was not desirable in a nation composed of many religious groups, that the pauper school idea was not in the interests of society, that free and general education was the natural right of children, and that only a public system could be free to teach whatever the welfare of the State demanded.

But they did not reckon on the strength of the opposition. Church schools feared that State schools would injure their progress and welfare. Schools with non-English-speaking pupils feared that State schools would supplant instruction in their own language. People without children resented being taxed for schools and others feared that State schools would lead to a State church. There was so much opposition that the Legislature in 1830 modified the Act of 1829, repealed the provisions for a township school committee, and abolished the licensing system. In 1831, the Legislature provided that parochial as well as private schools should receive portions of the appropriations from the State School Fund and gave townships the right to appropriate money "for the education of the indigent poor." Thus the church-controlled schools had negated the victories of those working for free public schools and set back for ten years the cause of common education for all supported with public funds.

These ten years were a period of "storm and stress" between the denominational groups and the advocates of the free school. Bishop Doane, of the Episcopalian Church, was about the only prominent religious leader who supported a free public school. Even he, at a later date, began to fear the "secular" influence of the common school and worked hard for the establishment of a complete system of Episcopal schools.

The Friends of Education worked untiringly to secure again the benefits of the Act of 1829 but support for the public school plan grew slowly. In 1835, the Governor said in his message to the Legislature:

> And first, as to our common schools, . . . they are confessedly inferior to those in some of our sister states. The branches taught are most ordinary, mere elements of information. There is no uniformity in the mode or system of instruction. . . . Many of our teachers are not well qualified. . . . They are not well compensated.

Finally, in 1838, an impressive convention was held in Trenton. Chief Justice Hornblower presided, and Bishop Doane presented an eloquent address urging the provision of a common school education for every child. "Let other states excel in commerce or in agriculture or in manufacture," he declaimed, "but let the staple of our State be mind. . . . Let our highest object be the State of our Common Schools, Colleges and Academies."

Resolutions were passed declaring that it is the duty of government to provide for the education of the children of its citizens, that present laws were defective, and that the people of New Jersey could not neglect a common school system. Other meetings were held with similar appeals. Finally, the Legislature in 1838 repealed the Law of 1831 and re-enacted all of the desirable features of the Act of 1829. The Act of 1838 increased the annual appropriations from the State School Fund to thirty thousand dollars, repealed the pauper school laws, required the election of the township school committee, required the committee to visit schools and make reports, authorized but did not require the county freeholders to elect county examiners to license teachers, and gave the school committees the right to examine teachers when the freeholders did not appoint committees for that purpose.

In 1839 the Trustees of the State School Fund made a

report by townships, as the Act of 1838 required. At that time there were 139 townships with over twelve hundred school districts. Reports were submitted from 89 townships comprising 940 school districts. In these districts there were 64,411 children between the ages of five and sixteen, of whom only 35,954 or about 55 per cent were attending school. Even though some children attended private schools and the count may not have been entirely accurate, it was a dark picture. The Trustees came to the conclusion that there were thousands of children not attending any school.

The Trustees distributed thirty thousand dollars from the State School Fund, and records indicated that the townships appropriated more than forty five thousand dollars to supplement this. It must be understood that the schools were not free and tuition charges were made ranging from $1.33 per child per quarter in Cape May to $2.43 in Burlington County. It was estimated that about one hundred and thirty seven thousand dollars was collected in tuition. When parents could not afford the charges, the school year was shortened. In Cape May it was only two months per year, in some counties five, ten in Burlington and Somerset, and eleven in Bergen. One problem was that the State School Fund was apportioned to the counties, and then to the townships, according to the taxes they paid, so that the wealthy townhisps received more and the poor ones less. Another strange requirement of the law set a limit on educational appropriations by the township at twice the amount received from the State. Objections to this were made by township officials. Many felt that if a township wished to appropriate more money, it should not be restricted by the State. This provision tended to force payment of more tuition instead of promoting free education. Only the "poor" could get education free and getting oneself classified as a pauper was humiliating. The Trustees showed their forward-looking attitude by saying in this report that "the first duty of a free state is to see that all of its children are provided with the means of education." It is interesting also, that in regard to the good record of Burlington County, they gave credit to (the Society of) Friends who, they said, "have always been liberal patrons of education."

How can one get an idea of what a school was like in the eighteenth and early nineteenth century? There seems to be evidence that not much improvement occurred until the end of this period. John Bodine Thompson, a teacher and the second agent of the State Teachers Association in 1856, describes the Center School about two miles from the "Head of the Raritan," which he attended in the 1820's, in his chapter on "Typical Schools" in David Murray's *History of Education in New Jersey*.

The first school of which I have any personal recollection was a counterpart of the "Dame school" of New England a hundred years before, save that the boys no longer wore knickerbockers. In summer, boys and girls alike went barefoot, and doors and windows were left wide open. Mosquitoes had not yet reached far inland. The school was held in "the old kitchen" which no longer served as such, though it was still a sort of storeroom for utensils used occasionally in a farmer's family. They had two half holidays a week. Monday morning the room was occupied by the tubs and kettles for the weekly washing. Saturday afternoons were devoted to the use of the scrubbing brush and mop to prepare for the Sunday School.

Such an improvised schoolroom was more comfortable than most of the country schoolhouses of the day. Professor Kalm, who visited his countrymen in New Jersey near the middle of the last century, commiserated their condition because they had no moss, such as grows so abundantly in Sweden, with which to stop the crevices of their log huts, but were compelled to use clay instead. My judgment is that the clay was better protection against the cold, and that the log schoolhouses and dwelling houses alike were made habitable only by its use. But before the middle of the century the log schoolhouse had given place to one built of boards, though innocent of plaster and paint; and it is quite doubtful whether it was as comfortable in winter as the log edifice which it supplanted. Indeed the country schoolhouse of the first half of this century would now be considered a disgrace in a civilized community. Usually it was perched upon the side of the public road, resting equally on it and the land of the adjacent owner, who quietly ignored the trespass. Claiming thus only a permissive existence and having no right to occupy space on earth, it seemed to feel its own insignificance. It squatted close to the ground, and, in one instance, at least, which I remember, hid its humble head beneath the branches of a huge red-apple tree. It was square, with the door in the middle of the side next the road.

The room was sixteen feet square. It had six windows of eight small panes each, with tight board shutters. These had once been provided with hooks and staples, but they had long since been broken off. In the absence of these, the shutters were fastened by propping against them stakes taken from the neighboring fence.

The atmosphere of the schoolhouse was peculiar. How sweet the smell of sap as it exuded from the green hickory logs laid across the stove to dry! How cold the room in the morning! How the stove smoked and sulked, and would not burn until toward noon, when the sun shone so warm that we could have done without the stove if we could only have been in the sunshine! The crevices in the floor served to let the slate pencils out and the cold air in, enough to keep our feet apparently in the regions of perpetual snow, while our heads were roasting in the climate of the torrid zone above. What treasures from pockets were confiscated from time to time and burned in the old stove—nuts, strings, song books, games, pin cases, etc.

Around the stove, we sat upon four long hickory slabs elevated upon the top of four poles. And on these scaffoldings, suspended like Mahomet's coffin between the heavens and the earth, without any support for the back or rest for the feet, the little martyrs of science were compelled to sit eight mortal hours a day, while in loud and rapid whisper they conned the column of words in Webster's spelling book from "Baker" to "Zany" inclusive.

In due time we were promoted to seats at the writing desk. This was a narrow board extending all around the room, inclined at an angle of 45 degrees, and covered with a variety of carved work and graven images. In and around these evidences of precocious talent was a deep groove, exemplifying what Dr.

Blair calls "the curve of beauty" through which we used to roll shot when the master's back was turned, though at imminent peril of our knuckles if detected.

It is difficult for the parents and children of the present day, accustomed as they are to well-designed buildings, comfortably heated, with furniture to fit the age of the child, and with a great variety of educational materials, to visualize the kind of school described by Thompson. The facilities of today are taken for granted with little thought for the struggles which have been made in the past one hundred years to arrive at our present standards.

If the schoolhouses of those days seem rudimentary to us, the methods of teaching and the life of the pupils must seem equally strait. That children should enjoy going to school was far from the thoughts of parents or teacher. Discipline was rigid, the rod was freely used, learning by rote was the accepted method. A vivid description of the school of the 1820's and 1830's was given by C. D. Deshler of New Brunswick in papers presented to the Historical Society of that city in 1892. In these he described in detail several schools which he had attended from 1826 on. His first teacher, a Mr. Spalding, was "muscular, virile, energetic, and full of vivacity. He was a strict disciplinarian; at my first coming to his school he used the ferule and the rod, but always in moderation and at length entirely discarded them." Deshler describes one occasion when he decided to whip a boy as large as he was, but in order not to humiliate him before the small children, Mr. Spalding took him upstairs to the lumber loft and administered the hiding before "those silent and unobserving witnesses."

Reading aloud was a frequent exercise and children of different ages took part together, being arranged in order of previous excellence. If a pupil cried "Challenge," he was permitted to point out the error which he claimed had been made in accent, emphasis, or pronunciation and if he made his case, he exchanged places with the reader. Thus a pupil of eight or ten might displace a boy of

These pictures of desks and chairs appeared in the Report of the State Superintendent of Schools for 1849. Comments indicated that the desk was made to accommodate two scholars, but that it could be made longer for a larger number. The pedestal was made of cast iron and the seat of wood. The pedestal was fixed to the floor by screws and was made to adjust to four different heights.

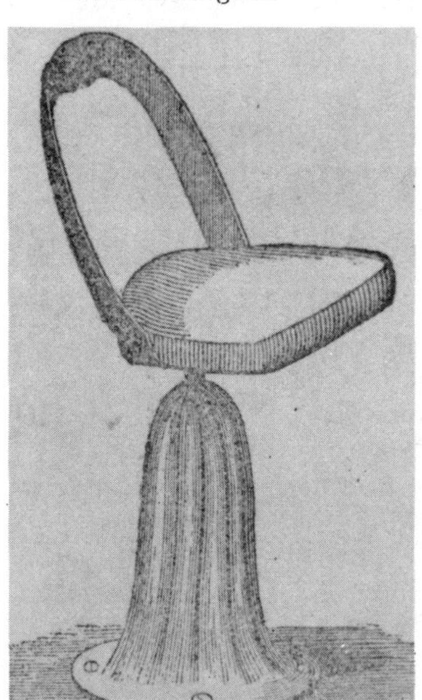

sixteen. Another popular drill was the "dictation" exercise. Here the pupil who had the highest standing in reading during the preceding week read slowly a piece from a standard work of literature. The pupils made notes as accurately as they could on their slates and when both sides of the slates were full were given time to transcribe what they had written to paper. Thus, pupils became expert in using original abbreviations and contractions similar to our shorthand systems.

Mr. Spalding not only believed in competition but he also knew how to make a boy appear ridiculous. If a boy was caught throwing a spit ball, he would be made to stand in a conspicuous place, chew paper, and then make motions with his hands as if throwing spit balls. On the other hand, this teacher would sometimes relieve tension by declaring a ten-minute recess outside for playing marbles or throwing snowballs.

Mr. Deshler described a woman teacher, Miss Saunders, as "sour, prim, sandy-haired, iron-visaged, lynx-eyed, and sharp-tongued." "So effective was her discipline that literally one might have heard a pin drop. We respected her though we feared her and regarded her with the same feelings of affection as one might have entertained for a pet dragon or tigress." He had one teacher, Mrs. Buckner, who apparently had some desire to entertain the pupils once in a while:

> Our studies and recitations which were mostly memoriter were interspersed with delicious intervals when Mrs. Buckner and her daughter sang or played for us or when in spring or summer, they sallied out with us into their garden and encouraged us to romp on the cool grass or under the shade of the lilacs or to wander among the flowers or the bee-hives.

One other teacher, Mr. Currie, had the habit of punishing a pupil by making him hold a book at arm's length, the weight of the book being in proportion to the seriousness of the offence committed. When the pupil's arm began to sag out of pain and weariness, he would administer a tap of the ferule underneath the arm to bring it back into position.

The pupils had their turn on the last day of the quarter when it was the custom to lock the schoolmaster in the schoolhouse while the pupils enjoyed a half holiday. Native teachers understood this and took it kindly. John Bodine Thompson tells us of one teacher from other parts who was not acquainted with this procedure; he administered such severe castigation for this prank that they remembered it for years. "But," said Mr. Thompson, "he was forced to emigrate to other regions in order to escape the ire of parents who never forgave him for his ignorance of the usual rites and ceremonies of the last day of the quarter."

To advance from the abominable physical conditions of the schoolhouses and from the ignorance and cruelty of the schoolmasters, most of whom were utterly untrained for teaching, the campaigners for better schools worked constantly to awaken the people to the needs and to persuade them to prepare better financial and administrative methods for attacking the problems. In 1844 a convention was held for the framing of a new constitution for the State. As finally adopted, the Constitution provided for the perpetuity of the State School Fund and for the distribution of the income for the "support of public schools." During the debates on this Article, proposals were made that the term "public schools" should be defined to exclude all sectarian schools, as difficulties had already arisen concerning the appropriation of money to the Society of Friends. The proponents of exclusion presented the dangers of assisting schools of a sectarian character but their proposals were voted down, thus paving the way for considerable argument in the next few years until the matter was settled in 1866 by the exclusion of all church-connected schools.

The period from 1800 to the adoption of the Constitution had witnessed significant progress in the campaign for the free public school and for the normal school. The legislative acts of the twenties and the thirties, the creation of the State School Fund, meetings held throughout the state, pamphleteering, and the organization of groups were all shaping public opinion to accomplish the desired ends. The debates concerning the proposed constitution and its adoption in 1844 also gave great stimulus to the campaign. The people were getting ready to accept the idea of the free public school and to put this idea into effect through proper legislative acts and administrative leadership.

III

THE CAMPAIGN FOR FREE PUBLIC SCHOOLS

IN 1845, a year after the adoption of the new Constitution, the proponents of free public schools achieved a decided success—the authorization by the Legislature for a State Superintendent of schools to be appointed by the Trustees of the State School Fund. Although the state superintendent was only a part-time officer, his professional duties included working for the advancement of schools and providing information for the public. In his report to the Legislature in 1847, the State Superintendent, Dr. T. F. King, a physician from Perth Amboy, discussed the general condition of the schools, the work done by examiners for teachers' licenses, the county associations of teachers, and the efficiency of teachers. Then he devoted considerable space to the "History, Nature and Advantages of Normal Schools."

He also discussed the problem of favoritism in the law of 1846 which made it possible for religious groups to receive public funds. Some had interpreted this Act as applying only to the schools maintained by the Friends, because this group required education as a part of their church discipline. His remarks foreshadowed the controversies which occurred during the next few years over this use of state funds. He praised the work done by religious societies for religious and moral instruction, but suggested that all sects should be treated alike and that freedom of religious worship should be promoted. Thus, he put himself on the side of those who would keep public education from favoring any one creed and who would promote the separation of church and state.

Reports from the township superintendents were also a requisite for receiving state aid. In the next few years, these reports gave frank and valuable appraisals to the state superintendent and the Legislature concerning the condition of the schools and the planning of local officials and citizens for needed improvements. Running through these reports are recurring complaints about the poor condition of the schoolhouses, the inadequate preparation of teachers, the indifference of the public, and the lack of funds. Once in a while a report would suggest that conditions were improving. But the need for a normal school and for meetings of teachers called "institutes" for the improvement of teaching was constantly stressed. There were also complaints that the state law did not clearly define what was meant by "education" in the use of state money. Apparently the interpretation was that the money should not be spent for school buildings. Consequently, contributions had to be depended upon for construction of buildings. Small wonder that the buildings were generally in miserable condition.

In 1848, the Legislature gave the township the right to use for the support of public schools the interest from the Surplus Revenue which had been received from the Federal government. Most counties assigned this money to the townships, and the amount was usually from thirty thousand dollars to forty thousand dollars annually. Now that the Federal debt is about three hundred billion dollars, it is interesting to note that at one time in our history the Federal government actually had a surplus to distribute.

Money from the State School Fund and from the Surplus Revenue was used, however, to pay a portion of the salaries of the district teachers and schoolhouses continued to be uncomfortable, often disgraceful.

The actual establishment of free schools grew slowly.

According to John Bodine Thompson [Agent of the State Teachers Association in 1856], a free school was started in Trenton in 1833, in the Masonic Hall on Front Street, which was presided over by Thomas J. Macpherson, father of the Speaker of the Assembly of 1896. Mr. Thompson says that it was not a municipal school, but it was successful. It was removed in 1838 to the upper floor of the jail adjoining the Trenton Academy, the school being in the upper portion and the jail in the basement. One might say that the entire building was occupied by "involuntary visitors."

Apparently the first free school, as we understand the term, was opened in 1844 in Nottingham under the leadership of Dr. Charles Skelton, often called the "Father of Public Schools." The act of the Legislature allowed the people of this township to raise six hundred dollars for the support of the school and five hundred dollars to erect a building. At the annual town meeting, the school committee recommended that the full sum allowed be appropriated, and in addition, that the interest on the surplus fund from the Federal government and the receipts from dog-tax be used for education. These proposals were carried by a large vote. Here, at least, the schools were not "going to the dogs," but were in part supported by the dogs. This seems to have been the first free public school in New Jersey since the end of Dutch dominion.

In 1850 the state superintendent reported that several townships had established free schools under special acts. Moreover, the schools had proved successful, and it was recommended that they should be extended as "the very principles of our government demand an educated people. . . . It is the only method of teaching our successors to appreciate their high responsibilities and destinies as republican citizens, and of qualifying them to perform with credit and usefulness the various duties which may devolve upon them." He reports the following communities as having free schools:

County	*Township*
Mercer	Nottingham and Trenton
Essex	Bloomfield, Newark, Plainfield
Camden	Camden
Cumberland	Bridgeton and Cohansey
Hudson	Hoboken, Jersey City, Van Vorst
Salem	Salem

In the rest of the State the average charge per quarter per pupil was $2.10, ranging from $1.96 in Morris County to $2.50 in Atlantic.

In the early 1850's, many of the township superintendents in their reports to the state superintendent urged the extension of *free* schools and the repeal of the law limiting the amount of money which a township could raise. Some felt that the State should raise the entire amount necessary and then distribute it to the townships. Some waxed eloquent concerning the need for more education. Daniel Cory of Warren County said:

> Let the children of the rich and poor be assembled in the same classroom, be instructed by the same teacher, recite in the same class, and know no distinction but that of knowledge and virtue. Charity schools are a disgrace.

As more free schools were organized, new difficulties were encountered. Many people in the townships who did not have children objected to being taxed. Town meetings became scenes of wrangling and controversy. Some districts used the money from the State and the township to run free schools for three or four months and then, when the money ran out, closed the schools or charged tuition to those parents who still sent their children. Other districts apportioned the money over the school year, charging the balance necessary for the operation of the school to the parents. Many superintendents advocated having the State appropriate all of the money needed for the operation of the schools so that local districts would thus avoid the many problems which arose in the local town meetings.

In 1851, supplements to the Act of 1846 were passed with several improvements. The annual appropriation from the State School Fund was increased to forty thousand dollars. Another forty thousand dollars was added from the general treasury. The money received was to be apportioned according to population. The law permitted local districts to appropriate funds not to exceed three dollars per child, made provision for building and repairing schoolhouses, and permitted the establishment of free schools on the favorable vote of two-thirds of the taxable inhabitants of a district. Said State Superintendent Phillips in 1852:

> Ample provision should be made to make easily accessible to every child, whatever his birth, circumstances or situation, the great fountains of knowledge and truth. As the summer cloud floats from the west to shed its treasures upon the thirsty earth, so should the common school be open and free to all who are athirst of knowledge, desiring to drink at its pure fountains and public opinion, that sovereign in representative governments, is in harmony with its principles.

But schoolhouses were still quite inadequate. Classes were often held in homes or in buildings erected by private enterprise. In 1852, Bordentown reported that not one of its seven schools met in a building owned by the township.

In 1853, however, Clara Barton, who later became famous as a Civil War nurse, came to Bordentown. She had been born in Massachusetts and educated in New York State, where she had also taught. She originally came to Hightstown to teach but, seeing a more urgent need in Bordentown, went there. She talked with urchins on the street, who told her that they did not have sufficient money for clothes or school. What Clara Barton saw and heard prompted her to go to the village trustees and ask to open a public school. At first she was refused, but she persisted and was finally granted a small building, where she taught for three months without payment. She was so successful and the school grew so rapidly that a larger building was erected containing eight rooms, where she taught until 1855, when her health became very poor. The original building is still standing; it was purchased as a shrine with pennies raised by the schoolchildren of New Jersey.

During this period some improvements were mentioned in the reports of the town superintendents. However, most reported that although conditions were improving, many were far from satisfactory. Some spoke of the demand of the people for better teachers and of increasing interest among parents. Others wrote of the general approval of the people in their townships of the recent acts of the Legislature, and of their desire for more improvements. Progress was slow and varied considerably in different sections of the State, but gains were being made and the people were being prepared for more progressive steps. Between 1852 and 1855, more committees for licensing teachers were appointed and the number of free schools grew so that for 1855, the state superintendent reported 29 townships with free schools.

In 1853, a convention of the teachers of the State was held in New Brunswick, with the result that a permanent association was effected. This is the foundation of the present New Jersey Education Association with its forty-nine thousand members. In 1855, the Association decided to employ an "agent" to work for the improvement of education. Christopher Columbus Hoagland was the first agent. He was followed in 1856 by the John Bodine Thompson whom we have already mentioned.

In 1854, eight teachers' "institutes" were held with a total attendance of over three hundred fifty teachers. An "institute" was a school for teachers, today it would probably be called a "workshop." Each institute lasted for several days and combined practical instruction in school procedures with general lectures. Money was appropriated by the State Legislature for these. In 1855, institutes were held in 13 counties and the reports were enthusiastic. In 1855, the Legislature appropriated money for the purchase of copies of Webster's *Unabridged Dictionary;* seven hundred were purchased to send to the common school districts.

One of the most interesting accounts of progress was given by the superintendent of schools in Elizabeth, in 1855 when it became a city. Conditions in the schools had not been good and the new commissioners made a thorough study, emphasizing in particular the cost of sending children to private schools. It was found that education could be provided much more cheaply by the city if proper arrangements were made. The commissioners conducted a publicity campaign, convinced the citizens, got an appropriation for a large brick schoolhouse, organized a graded school system to replace ungraded classes, and engaged good teachers. The superintendent said that the citizens were "ready to do their utmost to secure a triumphant success."

Many town superintendents felt that getting money from the citizens for free schools was too difficult. Said John Cox of Branchburg in 1855, "Raising money at town meetings for school purposes, is attended with much strife and opposition; voters generally voting from motives purely selfish." Many argued eloquently for more money from the State. Robert Freeman of Perth Amboy wrote in his report of 1856:

> The money appropriated by the state is scarcely more than an apology in comparison to the amount absolutely necessary to the proper education and training of our youth; and the making up of this amount is left to the cold mercies, and often the indifference of individual towns, some of whom are actually unable to raise anything like adequate sums sufficient to keep the school in operation during the year. My idea of a correct system of education is this; that the state legislature should appropriate to each school district a sum sufficient to support a good school at least ten months in the year, and that this amount shall be raised by a direct tax on all the taxable property of the state. We should then not see that miserable

condition of schools and school houses which now disgrace many parts of our state. The amount now required to be raised by individual town for the payment of teachers' wages, could then be appropriated to the erecting and furnishing of suitable school rooms, where children could be made comfortable and happy.

In many other reports arguments were advanced for greater State support. T. M. Bartolette of Hunterdon County wrote in 1859:

Every true Jerseyman must feel a tinge of shame mantling his cheek when he remembers how our State, with such great chances for adopting a good common school system, that will enable the most humble to avail themselves of knowledge, yet is so very far in the rear of other States inferior to us in resources.

The growth of the number of free schools was slow. In 1858 State Superintendent John H. Phillips reported there were 197 cities and townships in the state and in only 45 were all schools "free." In these cities and townships that year, there was a total of 1651 schools and 2103 teachers, showing that many had more than one teacher during the year. The average salary for male teachers was $393 per annum, and for female teachers, $237. From all sources in that year $537,772 was spent for the education of approximately 130,000 children, of whom 55,000 attended six months or less.

The advent of the Civil War impeded the progress being made in education naturally. Financial conditions were poor, and many men left to go into the army or to perform related duties, so the proportion of women teachers increased. In 1864 there were 806 male teachers and 1158 female teachers, whereas in 1857 there had been 1197 males and 885 females.

The state superintendent reported each year that conditions were improving slowly, but these improvements were mainly in the cities and large townships. These communities generally reported increased interest in schools, the advance of the graded system, improvement in the quality of the teachers, and the building of better schoolhouses. But the state superintendent took a gloomy view of conditions in general. In his report for 1864 he said:

> The reports from various sections of the State are not so encouraging as the friends of education can well desire. Indeed it is perfectly safe to remark that not more than ten percent of the youth of this State pursue a course of study sufficiently far as to accord a clear insight into the elementary subjects of Geography, Grammar and Arithmetic.

Over and over again, superintendents of smaller townships and rural areas complained bitterly of the lack of interest of parents, irregularity of attendance, inefficiency of teachers, the constant changing of textbooks, and of the miserable condition of many of the schoolhouses. The following report by Charles Morrow of Wantage, Sussex County, in 1864 is typical:

> There are in my township twenty-two schoolhouses, six very good, eight fair, and the remaining eight horrible, where the floors are broken through, and the children cluster in the corner during rain storms, and shiver as the wintry blasts whistle through. . . . Paint being a taxed article is scarce, while mats and scrapers are even more scarce; floors answer for spittoons and they are well used by teachers and pupils; furniture rude and sadly cut up—ventilation is complete though unpatented,—viz: through broken windows, dilapidated doors, roofs, and knot holes.

To assist the townships in erecting better buildings, the state superintendent in his report for 1865 included designs for schoolhouses—two types of one-story buildings to accommodate 48 pupils in a room 21′ x 36′; the third a building to accommodate 70 pupils, 25′ x 40′; and the fourth, a two-story building to accommodate 120 pupils —70 on the first floor and 50 on the second. Since these were recommended by the state superintendent, it can

The one-room Stelton School in Middlesex County as it appeared in 1882, is typical of nineteenth century schools all over New Jersey.

The interior of this Mount Pleasant school may seem dark and austere today, but the teacher has used specimens of the pupils' work for decorations.

be assumed that the number of pupils as stated was considered a normal load for a teacher.

Some of the cities reported that conditions were improving. For example, a Mr. Young, the Superintendent at Elizabeth, in 1864 wrote in his annual report, "The teachers are well educated; they love their work and perform it with zeal and ability. The citizens take a deep interest in their schools."

For several years, town superintendents complained in their reports to the state superintendent about the ineffectiveness of their jobs. They were elected by popular vote at town meetings, and paid one dollar for each day spent in work on school affairs. But they really had few duties except to act as treasurer and distribute to the districts money received from the State and appropriated by the township. They complained that the trustees of the districts had the power to hire teachers and manage the school affairs including the care of the schoolhouses. Furthermore, they by-passed the town superintendent by not requiring that teachers be licensed.

Town superintendent A. J. E. Romans, of Mantua, in writing of his problems in licensing teachers said in 1859:

> He must frequently license an applicant (probably after he has taught ten weeks of his time) when he knows as well as he lives that he is not qualified for the situation, and after visiting his school, and seeing almost every rule of order, discipline, and the systematic rules of experienced teachers violated, as well as common sense, then he feels alone; then he feels had he the power of Hercules, he would crush the Hydra-headed monster with his utmost power, satisfied like Samson, if he could die with his enemies.

In 1862 State Superintendent Ricord said in his annual report, "The examination of teachers of our public schools is, in a large number of cases, a perfect farce." In 1864, he pointed out that the rural districts did not have anything like the kinds of supervision being exercised in a few of the larger towns and cities. He recommended the establishment of county superintendents to visit schools, distribute laws, instructions, and reports, act with examiners in licensing teachers, assist in conducting teachers' institutes, keep records on file, organize normal classes for teachers, and acquaint the citizens with improvements needed.

In his report for 1865, Superintendent C. H. M. Angle of Frankford, Somerset County, says:

> The "well-to-do" trustee, without grumbling will pay his tailor $50. for an overcoat, or his wheelwright $300. for a carriage, both of which are quadrupled in price; yet if the "poor fellow" who is laboring to give his children an education, if that "ORNAMENT TO SOCIETY" at the "FORKS OF THE ROAD" should present him a bill for tuition, increased five percent, he would not only refues to cash it, but would at once call a "school meeting" and have the teacher dismissed for his INSOLENCE.

At a time when the average annual salary of male teachers was $478, and of female teachers $291, the complaint of the Superintendent seems justified.

A great step forward was made in 1866, when the State Board of Education was established by the Legislature. This Board consisted of the Trustees of the State School Fund and the Trustees and Treasurer of the Normal School, which was the institution established in Trenton in 1855 for the education of teachers. Important duties assigned to the Board were to appoint the State Superintendent of Public Instruction, recommend changes in the school law, and make an annual report to the Legislature. Another important step taken in 1866 was the repeal of the section of the school law which provided for the distribution of a portion of the public money to schools under the management and control of religious denominations. Thus all public moneys were reserved for the exclusive use of public schools. The appointment of Ellis A. Apgar as State Superintendent marked the beginning of an active crusade for the improvement of the schools and for "free" education.

The new state superintendent began to make a detailed study of the schools, and his report for the year 1866 provided the Legislature with statistics and recommendations. In that year out of 197,456 children between five and eighteen years of age, 39,557 had not attended school at all, and 48,854 had attended for three months or less. Out of 1972 schools, 1033 were reported as "free" but only 34 percent of these were open for the whole year. The number of male teachers was 821, and the number of female teachers 1478. The average cost of education for each child in the State was $3.59.

He asked every township superintendent to answer three questions in his report, as follows:

1. What changes should be made in our school laws and why?
2. What is necessary in order to secure a good degree of interest on the part of parents in regard to the education of their children?
3. How may we secure the services of active and efficient teachers?

He asked for two million dollars instead of the seven hundred fifty thousand dollars being expended and said that with this amount the public schools could be made much better than the private and denominational schools. "Some of the public schools found in our larger cities," Apgar wrote, "are the best in the world and the same course of elementary instruction can be given to every child in the State at an annual cost of ten dollars each."

The State Board of Education appointed a committee to consider what changes in the law were necessary. After six months of diligent study the committee recommended a systematic scheme of administration and of securing revenue. One of the most far-reaching of these recommendations was that of having county superintendents appointed by the State Board and the elimination of the township superintendents.

The Legislature passed a new "Act to Establish a System of Public Instruction." This repealed all previous acts and formulated an entirely new system. The State Board of Education authorized during the preceding year was retained, a plan for appointing county superintendents created, and the duties of the Board and the officers were newly defined. In 1867, Superintendent Apgar reported that although the new law had not had a fair trial, excellent results were already observable. Among these, he named consolidation of districts, more interest among teachers in improved methods of instruction, larger salaries, better system of licensing, increased uniformity of textbooks, tearing down of old schoolhouses and erection of new ones, and an additional number of free schools. It is interesting that at this time there was a determined effort to substitute the metric system of weights and measures for the previous system and Congress in 1866 passed Acts making the metric system lawful. How little progress had been made towards this end can be observed today! Superintendent Apgar thought that in a short time the metric system would be in general use and recommended that its study be introduced into all of the public schools.

He also made a strong argument for the right to tax the people for the support of public schools, basing much of his plea on the improvement of general prosperity and the well-being of the citizens of the State. So he wrote:

> Let all the children of the State be gathered in neat, comfortable, convenient and well furnished school houses, with whole-souled efficient teachers, to give them proper instruction, and we will add more to the wealth and resources of the State, and to the happiness, the comfort, the prosperity, and the virtue of the citizens, than if a gold mine should be discovered on every farm. . . . We want public schools in every community, and by public schools, I mean FREE schools; not schools HALF FREE as we have them. Education should no more be bought and sold than air and water.
>
> Let churches be built, let reform societies do their work, let all the agencies which have for their object the improvement

of mankind be encouraged and supported, but there is one cause which is the foundation of all reform, the corner stone of our government, the charter of our liberties, the secret of our prosperity in the past and the hope of our stability and success in the future, and that is the common school education for the whole people in the whole land without regard to race, color, condition, or sex.

This was the platform for the advocates of an efficient system of free public education in the struggle of the next ten years.

In 1871 State Superintendent Apgar wrote in his annual report:

There is a growing desire for free schools. . . . At present we have two sources from which we derive a general fund, the State appropriation and the township school tax. There are many objections to a township school tax which could be avoided by a State appropriation. Our public schools should not depend for their support upon a revenue, which a mere majority at town meeting, can any year withhold. Party interests, political issues, or the exertions of influential men opposed to public schools, will often defeat a school tax, and in consequence, the schools for the year must either be closed or tuition fees must be imposed upon those who attend.

The Legislature of that year passed an act making all of the public schools of the State entirely free. A fixed tax of two mills on a dollar for all property in the State was substituted for the uncertain township tax and trustees were prohibited from charging tuition fees. This State tax was distributed to the counties according to a school census of children between five and twelve years of age.

The Act gave a signal impetus to advance of education. It gave to the local districts sufficient money for teachers' salaries and fuel, and twenty dollars to each ditsrict for incidentals. The districts were given the power to raise money for school buildings and for repairs, and for teachers' salaries in the event that the money from the State did not meet the local needs. By passing this Act, the Legislature put on record the responsibility of the State for "free" education, even though in succeeding years local districts had to keep increasing their taxes in order to meet the growing demands for education, and the declining revenues from the State.

In 1871 another law was passed increasing the State School Fund by giving it all receipts from rental of land under water belonging to the State and the fund jumped from approximately $550,000 to $1,660,000 by 1879.

In 1874, the state superintendent made a determined effort to assist the smaller townships and rural areas in erecting schoolhouses. There had been much activity during the previous five years in replacing dilapidated structures. In that year, he reported that out of 1369 districts reporting, 29 had no schoolhouses at all but rented buildings, and 269 or 19 per cent were rated as "poor" or "very poor." Thirty-nine buildings were valued at $100 or less, 372 at between $100 and $500, and 396 at between $500 and $1000. Of all school buildings, 54 per cent were valued at $1000 and under.

In 1868 the total valuation of all school property was but $2,114,509 and this tripled in six years to $6,000,732. Through the help of an architect, the state superintendent presented in his annual report sketches for twenty-three different buildings ranging from a single-room structure to one with three classrooms, an assembly hall, and two small recitation rooms. He even included several pages of specifications to aid the local authorities in setting standards. It is interesting to note, however, that practically no progress had been made in reducing the size of classes, as most of the plans called for 45 to 50 pupils in a room, some even providing for as many as 72. All desks were the two-pupil type, screwed to the floor.

In 1876, certain amendments to the Constitution of 1844 were passed, of which the three following were of importance to education:

The Report of the State Superintendent of Schools for 1874 contained suggested drawings and brief descriptions followed by general specification, for 23 types of school buildings, for one to six-room schools. Here is a plan for a two-room school. One can seat 56 pupils, the other 48, at double desks. The rooms were separated by sliding blackboard partitions, and could be made into one large room for school assemblies. A ventilating shaft passed up through the belfry. It was estimated that this building would cost from $2500 to $2700.

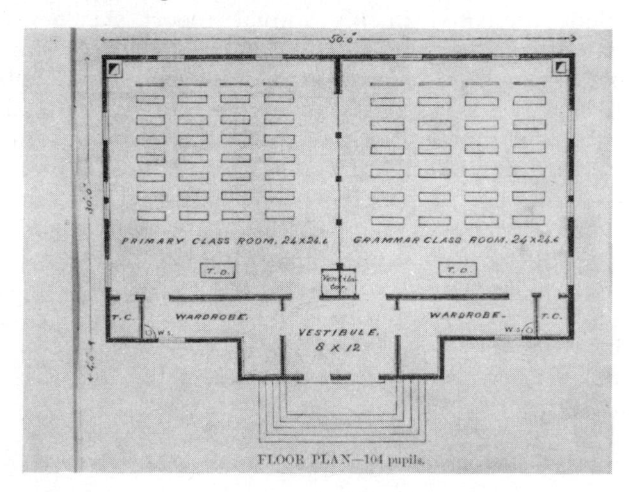

FLOOR PLAN—104 pupils.

No donation of land or appropriation of money shall be made by the State or any municipal corporation to or for the use of any society, association or corporation whatever.

The Legislature shall provide for the maintenance and support of a thorough and efficient system of free schools for the instruction of all the children in this State between the ages of five and eighteen years.

The Legislature shall not pass private, local or special laws providing for the management and support of free public schools.

It had taken one hundred years after Washington's victory over the Hessians at Trenton to achieve the fundamentals of a free public school system for the education of all the children of all the people. In 1876, the State had a Constitutional guarantee of public education, and statutes providing for adequate State administration through a State Board of Education and a State Superintendent of Public Instruction, efficient county administration through the county superintendents, a large amount of State financial subsidy through the State School Fund and the two-mill tax, and power of the local districts to tax themselves for additional amounts desired and for schoolhouses. A normal school had been established, efficient certification of teachers was provided for, and teachers' institutes were well established. Much remained to be done but the basic principles existed.

Maurice Beerley, County Superintendent of Cape May, said in his annual report of 1876, "The last decade has been more fruitful and exhibited more energy and advancement in education than we find in the nine decades of the last century that preceded it." And another, William L. Dickinson of Hudson County, said in the same year, "Ten years of growth and improvement have so changed the aspect of our schools within and without that one who should return after a prolonged absence from a distant land to revisit here the schools of his boyhood, would find it hard to believe that they were the same or in the same country." The spirit of democratic progress was in the air. A new era was at hand.

Actually the achievements of the decade from 1866 to 1876 were the culmination of a campaign which had been waged ever since the beginning of the century. Many groups and many individuals were involved. They fought with amazing zeal and with the spirit of missionaries devoted to a great cause. They were sustained by the belief that the new democracy must be undergirded by the intelligence and education of all of its citizens, no matter how lowly. They might have been naïve in their faith that education would reduce crime and empty the prisons. But they were sound in their fundamental conviction that education would open the doors of opportunity to every man and give him the chance to use his talents to their utmost capacity. They were laying the foundation for the kind of state in which race, religion, and economic status would not be a barrier to those who had the ability to improve themselves and contribute to the common good. By establishing the common school on a firm basis, they were preparing the way for greater opportunities in the development of the high school and college.

Another contribution which they envisioned for the common school was the transformation of the European newcomers into American citizens who would share the mores and culture of the new democratic society. As the nineteenth century developed, the school became the "melting pot" which helped to make an unique person—an "American"—devoted to the ideals of freedom, to universal education, and to the opportunity for every person to rise from the bottom to the top if he has the requisite ability. Decades later, when increasing numbers of people came from cultures quite different from those of the early settlers, these foundations proved to be of inestimable value.

During the last quarter of the nineteenth century, steady progress was made in the erection of schoolhouses, grading of schools, development of courses of study, and education of teachers. The abolition of the district system and the organization of these districts under the townships in 1894 expedited the rate of advance. The township system eliminated the divisiveness of the former "district" organization and established units large enough to operate efficiently. Free textbooks also came. Compulsory education laws were passed although they were not implemented by effective attendance officers until about the second decade of the twentieth century when the present requirements of school attendance from ages seven to sixteen were set. Figures reported in 1899 showed that of a child population in New Jersey of about four hundred fifty-five thousand between the ages of five and eighteen, about 70 per cent were in public schools, 10 per cent in private schools, and a shocking 20 per cent in no schools at all. Many of these were probably in the upper years and had not continued beyond the elementary school, or the eighth grade as we know it now.

At the end of the century, male teachers averaged $800 per year and female teachers about $450 which was an increase of about 20 per cent since 1875. To evaluate these figures in terms of the present value of the dollar is difficult. The government's Price Index indicates that a dollar in 1913 would have bought three times what it would buy in 1960. Certainly the amounts given in 1900 would have to be multiplied by four or five to get a comparison with the present day. Teachers were underpaid but some increases had been granted.

Although remarkable advances had been made, particularly in the second half of the century, people were beginning to wonder if the schools were adequate to meet the new demands emerging from the impact of science and technology. Great changes in industry, commerce, and other aspects of living were around the corner. There were stirrings of a new philosophy of education destined to produce great changes in the relation of education to society. Feeble demands were made for the professionalization of the administration of education. Teacher preparation and the curriculum were scrutinized to determine what advances must be made. To understand the criticisms and the proposals for improvement, the development of these two aspects of education now needs to be examined.

IV

THE TEACHER PROBLEM

IT HAS ALREADY BEEN NOTED that in the colonial days, in addition to the schools maintained by the religious sects, two other kinds of schools developed, the "Dame school" in a home and the district school maintained in a building, often contributed by a group or by an individual and made available for school uses. Parents had to pay tuition in the "Dame school" which was really a private school. In the district school, maintained by the voters, fees were also paid, sometimes supplemented by money voted by the citizens. The teacher in the Dame school was the matron of the household who had enough education to teach the pupils the rudiments offered. The district school had great difficulty in finding teachers and would often advertise in the newspapers for a suitable instructor. The following, which appeared in the *Pennsylvania Gazette* on December 11, 1755, is typical:

> Wanted——A sober person that is capable of teaching a school; such an one, coming well recommended, may find encouragement by applying to David Stratton of Evesham in the County of Burlington, West New Jersey.

The Trustees hired the teachers who, without examination or license, started on the appointed day to "keep school" as their work was called. The schools that could pay the largest compensation got the best teachers, and the poorer districts had to take what came to them.

Teachers would often stay for a single quarter and then leave for a better position or some other kind of work, so that a given school might have several teachers in a year. No marked changes occurred in this general scheme through the entire eighteenth century except that a few teachers educated in New England came into the schools of New Jersey. These men had sometimes had part or all of a college education but had had no special training for teaching.

Another type of school known as the Lancasterian School made its appearance in the first quarter of the nineteenth century. It derived its name from Joseph Lancaster, an Englishman who invented and promoted the idea of having a large number of pupils under one teacher, with older, brighter boys being assigned as "monitors" to hear groups of about ten younger children recite their lessons. The teacher would instruct the monitors and then a monitor would instruct a group according to what he had learned. Such a method obviously depended on rote recitations of facts that could be recorded and given to the monitor to check. Classes were inexpensive and thus appealed to the taxpayer. Lancaster came to Mount Holly in 1818 and in the following year several teachers trained in New York came to the schools of Mount Holly. Other schools in southern New Jersey as well as in New Brunswick and Newark adopted the plan. Although it did not have the merits of an efficient school program, the Lancasterian system did increase the growing appeal of free schools and it demonstrated the need for improvement in the education of teachers.

It has already been noted that the campaign for professional education of teachers was a companion of that for the free public school. As early as 1828, John Maclean of Princeton, in a *Lecture on a School System for New Jersey,* urged the creation of a school "to educate young men for the business of teaching." After the establishment of the State School Fund, the required reports of the town superintendents constantly reiterate the difficulties of securing decently prepared teachers and the urgency of having a normal school. Such demands grew more insistent during the 1840's. Horace Mann had been elected Secretary of the Massachusetts State Board of Education and within two years (1839) he was successful in having established the first state normal school in Lexington, Massachusetts. With him and with many of his followers in New England as well as New Jersey, the campaign for proper education of teachers was a spiritual crusade. They saw the cause of public education as a sacred cause, a grand campaign for democracy and humanity.

Said Horace Mann at the dedication of the Bridgewater Normal School in Massachusetts in 1846:

> I believe Normal Schools to be a new instrumentality in the advancement of the race. Neither the art of printing, nor the trial by jury, nor a free press, nor free suffrage can long exist, to any beneficial and salutary purpose, without schools for the training of teachers. Coiled up in this institution, as in a spring, there is a vigor, whose uncoiling may wheel the spheres.

In New Jersey complaints about the lack of preparation of teachers were epitomized by Christopher Hoagland of Hillsboro in Somerset County in this report to the state superintendent in 1849:

> From the examination of nearly 300 teachers, we had occasion to observe that while many were extremely defective in elemental knowledge, and depended, in their attempts to instruct, upon the textbook in their own hands, a far greater number were almost unaware that there is any such thing as tact in teaching, supposing that to keep tolerable order in school by a salutary fear of the rod, to hear a class read a given number of times in a day, to help a pupil do a sum in arithmetic, to hear a lesson imperfectly recited in geography, and to keep a writing book passably clean of blots, make up the sum total of a man's claim to be considered a good teacher. Not one in fifty had read any book or treatise on the art and science of teaching, and many had never heard that there were any such works in existence.

Town superintendents in the forties and fifties constantly complained of the inadequate preparation of teachers and of the need of a normal school. From Clinton came this pungent statement, "There is but little attention paid to the qualification of a teacher, provided he is a clever fellow, and will work cheap." Said the Superintendent of Perth Amboy:

"Give us," the parents say, "abler teachers and we will support them." . . . But where shall we get teachers, is a question of no easy solution. Our state needs an efficient Normal School, to meet the growing demands for teachers of a higher order.

From Rockaway: "I almost despair of being able to bring about the very desirable result of having every school supplied with a thoroughly competent teacher."

The Belvidere superintendent wrote eloquently concerning the ability of the State to support a normal school. "Who shall establish such an institution?" he asked, and then answered his question:

None more worthy than New Jersey herself. New Jersey, FREE FROM DEBT, relieved from taxation, rich in agricultural resources, situated between two of the best markets in these United States, and perfectly easy of access—what is there to hinder her from adding another wreath to her already immortal fame?

In many of the counties the freeholders neglected to appoint examiners, as the law provided, and when the district trustees hired teachers, several weeks would often elapes before the teacher went to the town superintendent to be licensed. Obviously, the latter could hardly refuse, except in very unusual cases.

As a substitute for an institution for the education of teachers, associations of teachers were formed and county institutes organized. The first meeting was held in Somerville in the fall of 1851 with speakers from Connecticut and Massachusetts as well as local people. It was attended by 62 teachers and was said by the state superintendent to have been a "glorious meeting." Specific instruction was given concerning teaching methods and there were general lectures on duties of teachers, how to handle problems of discipline, and accomplishments which should be expected of pupils.

Christopher Columbus Hoagland had been primarily responsible for this institute and in 1855 he was appointed the first agent of the State Teachers Association. Dr. Hoagland was to visit all parts of the State and "in every practical way to labor for the establishment of a normal school." Prominent men who were very influential in the campaign for a normal school were principal John T. Clark of New Brunswick, editor David Naar of Trenton, State Superintendent John H. Phillips, Richard S. Field of Princeton, and Governor Rodman M. Price.

The State Teachers Association awarded a prize of twenty dollars to Principal Clark for his essay on education in the State. In it he said:

> Surely, if anyone needs professional preparation before entering upon his duty, it is the teacher. We must have a State Normal School, with a Model School attached, wherein our young men and women shall be fitted for teaching, in the same manner as persons are fitted for other professions—viz. by an apprenticeship, as a business for life.

After the establishment of the first state normal school in Lexington, Massachusetts, in 1839, three others were opened in Massachusetts, one in Providence, Rhode Island, one in New Britain, Connecticut, one in Albany, New York, and one in Ypsilanti, Michigan. The New Jersey campaigners used letters praising the work of these institutions and worked on the pride of their fellow citizens not to lag behind their sister states. Teachers from New England who came to New Jersey schools were also influential in the establishment of such a school.

Between 1850 and 1855, several conventions were held of both laymen and teachers for the promotion of a normal school. Resolutions were passed and petitions sent to the Legislature. Finally, in February, 1855, a bill was passed and signed by Governor Price. Several communities made bids for the school site, but it was finally located in Trenton, and opened October 1, 1855, in a temporary building with 15 students registered. The permanent building on North Clinton Avenue, financed by citizens of Trenton, was occupied in 1856.

In his report for 1855, State Superintendent John H. Phillips, commenting on the establishment of the State Normal School, had this to say about its meaning for education in the State:

It is a remarkable fact that no state in the union, nor nation of the old world, has perfected its system of public instruction without schools for the training and education of teachers, established and maintained by public authority; and it is no less remarkable that with nearly three hundred such schools now in successful operation in this country and in Europe, there is not on record a single instance, where the

Trenton Normal School Building opened in 1856 and Model School Building opened in 1857. Commenting on the Normal School Building, Principal Phelps wrote, "In all its appointments this building leaves little to be desired in respect to simplicity, convenience, and adaptation to the purposes for which it was designed."

experiment has been tried under liberal legislative patronage, of the abandonment of this agency in providing good teachers for the public schools.

William F. Phelps was appointed principal. He had graduated from the New York State Normal School in Albany and had taught there for several years. The tradition of "selective admission" was established in the first year, as entrance examinations were given on November fourth (which was also Thanksgiving Day) to those who had reported on October first. Tests were given in arithmetic, geography, English grammar, reading, spelling, and penmanship. Some of the questions are recorded in the diary Mary Jane (Sergeant) Larison kept from October 1, 1855 to April 2, 1856, and they indicate how much emphasis was put on exact knowledge and how little on application of this knowledge to social situations. Many of our present-day high school graduates would find it difficult to answer the arithmetic and geography questions. All of the 15 students who had been in the school since October first and the date of this examination were allowed to remain.

Phelps believed that those who were admitted to the school should possess a good academic education, and he visualized the school as one which would train teachers in the theory of teaching and give them initial experience in the classroom. It was not possible to operate within this framework, because the students who had been admitted were scholastically deficient in elementary subjects and much time had to be spent in teaching them the subject matter they were going to teach.

Some idea of what was being taught in the elementary schools of that era is gained by studying the curriculum of the Normal School. Under "English" was listed work in Sounds, Spelling, Reading and Elocution, Grammar, Composition, and the Art of Debate. As "Graphics" were listed Penmanship and Bookkeeping; Object, Map, and Mechanical Drawing. As "Mathematics" the following were studied: Oral and Mental Arithmetic, Written Arithmetic, Practical Mathematics, Mathematical Geography, and Elements of Algebra and Geometry. "Natural Science" was composed of Descriptive and Physical Geography, Human and Comparative Physiology, Elements of Natural Philosophy and Chemistry. The students, under the heading of "Ethics," studied Moral Philosophy, Natural Theology, the Constitutions of the United States and New Jersey, School Law of New Jersey, and the History of the United States. The "Theory and Practice of Teaching" consisted of Intellectual Philosophy, Study of School Systems, Lectures on Education and Details of Teaching and Practice in the Model School. Vocal music was given throughout the course.

Apparently no attention was paid to ancient or European history, not much to science as we know it, very little to psychology or child study except as it came into practice teaching. Art is not mentioned except in relation to drawing maps and objects.

In her diary, Mary Jane Larison put down the program of one of the classes in the Model School for a forenoon. The entire time was devoted to arithmetic, spelling, writing, reading, and geography.

One of the strong elements of the program introduced into the Normal School was observation of good teaching and practice with pupils in a typical classroom. During the first year, a so-called Model School was opened on the first floor of the Normal School. Later, having proved its usefulness, the Model School occupied a building of its own adjacent to the Normal School. This was the beginning of a policy which has grown in importance to the present day. The school used for the purpose of giving actual experience to the teacher-trainees have been called "Training Schools," and later "Demonstration Schools," and sometimes "Laboratory Schools." Whatever they were called, observation and study of good teaching in such a school, and practice in the school or in cooperating schools of the State, have been keystones of the teacher education program in New Jersey in all its normal schools and in the development of the teachers colleges.

The period from 1855 to 1865 was one of slow advance in some fields and of difficulties caused by the Civil War. The original act had authorized the normal school for a period of five years. Despite some opposition to it, the Act was renewed in 1859 for another five years. A class of 32 (21 "ladies" and 11 "gentlemen") was graduated in 1858 and enrollment grew so that in 1860 there were 58 students (32 women and 26 men); but in 1861 there were only 18 women and 13 men because of the Civil War and attendant financial difficulties. As a matter of fact, many students left and went into teaching without completing the course. The state superintendent reported that by the end of 1858, 264 pupils had been "admitted and instructed" at the normal school, of whom 32 had received the diploma and 114 had stayed for longer or shorter periods and had left the school without graduating. Most of those who left before graduating were teaching.

But the reports of the town superintendents indicate that a very large majority of them had high hopes that the normal school would in time provide them with well-prepared teachers. Several said that they could get some good teachers from those who showed up with training in other states or with some kind of advanced education. Many, however, echoed John Ford of Hanover who wrote, "We are still suffering from a scarcity of teachers of the right kind and from the still more frequent changes of those we had. It is becoming a more and more serious question—What are our schools to do?"

Ephraim Bateman of Fairfield said:

> The teachers employed, I regret to say, are too many of them young and inexperienced; they resort to teaching as a temporary expedient, intending to abandon it as soon as a more lucrative situation shall offer. They are, alas! often lamentably deficient in much that goes to constitute a good teacher.

The campaign for the establishment of a state normal school gave an impetus to efforts in some cities to give professional training to their teachers, even if it had to be on a part-time basis. Newark started Saturday classes for its teachers in 1855. This was the foundation for what in 1878 became a one-year training school and a two-year school in 1888. It contained as a city normal school until 1913 when it became a State normal school. Paterson started evening and Saturday classes in 1855. In 1882 this school had its first class of high school graduates; in 1897 it went on to a two-year course and continued as a city normal school until taken over by the State in 1923. Jersey City in 1856 began Saturday classes which lasted until 1879 when training classes were held in the high school. In 1900, a two-year curriculum was established which continued until the State built the Jersey City Normal School in 1929.

Although these early teacher-training classes were rudimentary, they served the purpose of establishing the case for professional training, they encouraged teachers to continue studying while they were teaching, and thus they kept their curricula close to the actual needs of the persons who attended.

In 1867, rules were set up by the recently created State Board of Education for teacher certification, in both county and State. Apparently impressed with past laxity, the state superintendent and the State Board decided on rigid requirements as a means for improvement of teaching. Three certificates were set up for the counties: First, Second, and Third. The Second and Third were good only in the county where issued, but the First was good for the entire State. Candidates for the lowest or Third Grade Certificate had to be sixteen years of age and pass examinations in orthography, reading, writing, geography, practical arithmetic, and English grammar. For a Second Grade Certificate, a candidate had to be seventeen years old, have taught for one year, and have passed the examinations prescribed for the Third Grade Certificate with the addition of History of the United

States, Bookkeeping, and Theory and Practice of Teaching. For the First Grade Certificate, candidates had to be eighteen years of age, with two years of teaching experience, and have passed the examinations prescribed for Third and Second Grade Certificates plus examinations in Physiology, English Composition, Algebra, The Constitution of the United States, and the School Law of New Jersey. Ten questions were prescribed for each test. That these examinations were difficult is attested to the fact that even after ten years (1876), 25 per cent of the 2122 candidates who took the tests failed to qualify.

In addition to the county certificates, the State Board of Examiners also granted First, Second, and Third Grade State Certificates, for teaching anywhere in the State. Candidates for the Third Grade Certificate had to be nineteen years old, with three years of teaching experience, and take examinations in Spelling, Reading, Penmanship, Bookkeeping, Geography, English Grammar, Arithmetic, Algebra, Geometry, Trigonometry, History and Constitution of the United States, General History, Rhetoric, Mental Philosophy, English and American Literature, Natural Philosophy, Chemistry, Geology, Botany, Physiology, Theory and Practice of Teaching, and the School Law of New Jersey. Now, in 1867, for the first time since its establishment in 1855, the graduates of the normal school were given this Certificate without examination and non-graduates were given a temporary license good for one year.

Candidates for the Second Grade Certificate had to be twenty-one years of age, with four years of experience, and take the same examination as for the Third Grade Certificate, but the Certificate granted was for five years instead of four. Candidates for the First Grade Certificate had to be twenty-five years old, with five years of experience. The same examinations as for Second and Third Grade Certificates had to be taken with the addition of examination in any three of sixteen pedagogical texts offered. Each candidate also had "to deliver a lecture to a class on some subject previously assigned by the Examiners, and to draw up a plan for organizing the schools of some large city." This license was good for life, and one might say that anyone passing all these hurdles deserved it. All tests were marked on a scale of 100, and no license could be granted to a teacher whose general average fell below 70, or to anyone whose special mark in any one of the studies required for the Third Grade County Certificate was less than 70.

In the ensuing years, some districts conducted their own tests for teachers in addition to those required for certification. The examination below was used in Hamilton Township District #1, in 1877, and was recorded in the minutes of the Trustees. Sixteen candidates took this examination for one vacancy. It would be interesting to find out how many seniors in the State colleges and schools of education in the State at the present time could answer the questions in arithmetic, geography, and grammar in this test. It is quite obvious that, in that day, specific knowledge was considered a prime necessity.

1. a. Have you a Teacher's Certificate, or Diploma?
   b. From whom and what date?
   c. What were your averages?
2. a. What experience have you had in teaching?
   b. When? Where? Grade?
3. In what grade would you prefer to teach? Why in that grade?
4. Will you accept a position as a teacher in any room in our schools, commencing next Monday, April 30th?
5. Would you be likely to be often absent from school on account of ill health, or other causes?
6. What mode of punishment would you adopt for misconduct?
7. What incentives for study would you adopt?
8. How would you teach morals and good manners in school?
9. What special rules would you prefer to adopt in the government of your school?
10. How should a teacher spend her time out of school hours?
11. Give the principles of Roman Notation and express 1745 by this method.
12. What part of one dollar is one-fifteenth of thirteen and a quarter cents?

13. If a brick is 8 inches long, 4 inches wide, and 2 inches thick, how many bricks will there be in a pile 32 feet long, 4 feet high and 18 inches thick?
14. Write a Sight Draft.
15. Give the punctuation marks, their names and use.
16. Define Simple, Complex, Compound sentence, and give an example of each.
17. How it rains! Analyze the sentence and parse each word.
18. By what states is Illinois bounded?
19. Name the states bordering on each side of the Mississippi River.
20. What waters lie between Turkey in Europe and Turkey in Asia?
21. Through what Lakes and Rivers would you pass in going from Chicago to the Atlantic Ocean?

By 1880, the twenty-fifth anniversary of the establishment of the normal school at Trenton, distinct advances could be detected in the professional education of the teachers of the State, but much remained to be accomplished. Enrollment had grown from the 15 entrants of 1855 to 199 in 1880. But only 36 are recorded as graduating in that year, as many left and went to teaching before graduation. Several city training schools were in operation and the system of requiring either county or State examinations for certification was well established.

Although there were a few changes, this system of county and State certification remained in force until the reorganization of the State Department of Education in 1911. Cities were also given the right to issue certificates good within their school systems. The graduates of the normal school received a temporary certificate, which was good for life after the satisfactory completion of two years' teaching. In 1908 it was reported that of 10,602 teachers, 2759 had county certificates of various grades, 3566 State certificates, and 4277 city certificates. That it was not easy to pass the examination is shown by the fact that, in the same year, out of 1745 candidates for county certificates, 1136 were granted certificates and 609 failed. The principles of certification had been advanced and the ground laid for new rules more in tune with the advancing standards of education and the increasing differentiation of school positions.

That much had to be done to provide well-trained teachers for the entire State is shown by the small number who completed the normal school course in 1880. Although there was a total enrollment of 291, only 37 graduated from both the February and June classes. W. A. Whitehead, President of the Board of Trustees, said in his report of that year, "The demand for graduates is increasing as they generally not only give satisfaction but manifest superior abilities for work in the schoolroom and make full returns for their obligations to the State." The 37 graduates came from 13 counties: Mercer (7), Burlington (3), Somerset (3), Essex (3), Bergen (3), Gloucester (2), Sussex (2), Hunterdon (2), Warren (2), Cumberland (2), Union (2), Middlesex (1), Salem (1), and 4 were listed as out of state. Eight counties were not represented at all. It is evident from the reports of the superintendents that most of the graduates went to the cities and large towns and that the rural areas were still suffering from a lack of adequately trained teachers. In 1881 State Superintendent Apgar reported that out of 3486 teachers in the State, 238 were graduates of the normal school and 138 others had had some work there. This meant that approximately 7 per cent of the teachers employed in that year were graduates and 4 per cent had left to teach before graduating, thus making 11 per cent in all who had had teacher preparation in the normal school.

The principles of teacher education had been established and a certification method authorized to set up standards for those who did not attend a normal school. It took many more years to secure sufficient facilities to educate even for two years beyond the high school level the number of teachers needed by the State each year, and to establish a demand backed up by proper salary which would induce young people to become teachers and secure the proper training for this profession.

V

THE SCHOOL COURSE OF STUDY

IN THE EARLY SCHOOL, the first book to be widely used following the "hornbook" was *The New England Primer.* The "hornbook" was really not a book but a small flat board with a handle. On this was pasted a sheet of paper containing the letters of the alphabet, the vowels, combinations of vowels and consonants, and certain religious items. Over this was a strip of transparent horn held by a narrow strip of thin metal and nails.

The New England Primer had the famous rhymed couplets starting with "In Adam's fall/We sinned all" through the alphabet to "Zacchaeus he/Did climb the tree/His Lord to see." Also it contained the "Shorter Catechism." This book was first advertised in 1691 and was widely used in New Jersey. An importation from England also widely used was Dilworth's *A New Guide to the English Tongue,* really a combination speller, reader, and grammar. In 1783 Webster's *Speller* came out. It was much more than a speller, as it contained material relating to pronunciation, the diacritical marks over the vowels, and analysis of sounds and the common combinations of letters which make words. So it began with words like "hem—gem," then "sit—wit," "rap—map," and so on. Then it went to longer words in their families. It also contained short stories and fables and was thus a reader as well as a speller.

Soon after 1800, so-called readers began to be published. Most of these were based on moral lessons and some had rather elegant illustrations to make a lasting impression on the "tender minds" of children.

Murray's *English Reader,* published in 1808, had in a chapter of one book the following sections:

1. The importance of a good education
2. On gratitude
3. On forgiveness
4. Motives to the practice of gentleness
5. A suspicious temper, the source of misery to its possessor
6. Comforts of Religion
7. Diffidence of our abilities, a mark of wisdom
8. On the importance of order in the distribution of our time

What did people consider important in their schools? Some ideas can be obtained from the "Rules and Regulation" of 1825 for the government of the Center School, about two miles northwesterly from the "Head of the Raritan," as described by John Bodine Thompson. Those relating to actual instruction were as follows:

1. As spelling is the foundation of good reading, and therefore essential to the school, it shall be the duty of the teacher every morning and evening at the close of school, to make all those who can spell or stand in regular order and to spell out of the book, each his word in order as the teacher shall think proper.
2. It shall be the duty of the teacher to make all the scholars say three lessons to him in every half day, besides the spelling lesson, except such as shall cipher; they shall say one reading lesson in each half day.
3. It shall be the duty of the teacher to see those who write keep their copy books neat and clean, that they may be shown to the trustees of the school on the last Saturday of every quarter, if not every month.
4. It shall be the duty of the teacher to make the cipherers commit well to memory the different rules of arithmetic, and when the trustees attend to examine them on said rules, if they request it.
5. It shall be the duty of the teacher to refrain from all spirituous liquors while engaged in this school and not to

enter the house when intoxicated nor to lose time through such intemperance.

Reading, writing, and particularly spelling were the chief items of instruction. Some apparently were introduced to arithmetic, but the mention of "rules" indicates that much of the instruction was of a routine nature emphasizing memorization. There is evidence that some teachers got into trouble through gambling and drunkenness. On the other hand, although pay was low and professional recognition hardly existed, some considered teaching a serious calling, pursued it for many years, and were highly thought of by their pupils.

The trustees of the State School Fund felt the responsibility of recommending measures for the general improvement of the education of the people as well as reporting on the distribution of the fund. This is shown in their first report in 1839 in which they noted that reports did not indicate the townships had spent any of the money received from the State for books. The trustees, since they found there were large sections of the State without public libraries, supplied information about publication in New York of a series of books designed to form a district library. This series embraced fifty volumes and could be purchased with a "neat bookcase" for twenty dollars. In a supplementary statement, the titles were listed. They included the history of Europe and of the United States, books about Indians, the Chinese, astronomy, Palestine, books on birds, insects and animals, Plutarch's *Lives,* lectures on general literature, and other subjects. How such a list could be purchased for twenty dollars is a wonder. In 1848, the state superintendent had much to say about the advantages of district libraries, with great praise for New York and what it had done in this area. The superintendent recommended strongly that the townships place "within the reach of every individual, both young and old, male and female, parent and child, a large and judiciously selected assortment of books, comprising the most approve and standard scientific, literary, and other works, in every department of useful and practical knowledge."

The first subject to be added to the three R's and spelling was geography. Jedediah Morse of Massachusetts in 1785 published a "Geography" which was revised at later dates and widely used. It was a ponderous book without a single illustration. The subject was factual, astronomical, physical, natural, and political geography, with few of the social implications commonly taught today. There were many definitions and much memory work on capitals, boundaries, and principal products. By the middle of the nineteenth century, because of the influence of the Swiss educational philosopher, Johann Heinrich, Pestalozzi and others, more attention was paid to out-of-door observation and the substitution of human aspects for statistics.

Professor Arnold Guyot at the Trenton Normal School, later a professor at Princeton University was well known in this field. Notes on his lectures, in the Diary of Mary Jane Larison for 1856, show how he related his work on climate, winds, and other natural phenomena to the human and social conditions of the regions being studied. Guyot was a disciple of Pestalozzi and one of the first of a group of teachers who came to America from Switzerland.

History as such was not studied until the second quarter of the nineteenth century, and then about all that was considered important was the history of the United States. Even after the Civil War, when this study became more popular, its chief materials were national heroes and the glories of the Revolutionary War. Until the end of the century, the development of our own West was of sufficient moment, and the rest of the world seemed quite unimportant.

Even prior to the organization of the normal school at Trenton, changes had been taking place in the curriculum of the schools and in the textbooks used. Many teachers came from New England and New York, bringing with them new ideas about what should be taught.

New textbooks were being introduced, too, particularly after 1840. Often this brought complaints, either from those interested in keeping alive the parochial schools who found the new books too "secular," or from frugal parents who resisted buying new books with the coming of every new teacher. Readers, although still quite religious in nature, began to offer more interesting material related to more worldly affairs. The new arithmetic books recognized that the pupil was capable of thought and conesquently some of the mechanical methods of drill were abandoned.

Some idea of what was considered important then in the daily program of the schools may be gleaned from the report of the town superintendent of Hamilton Township to the state superintendent in 1856. Of the 19 rules which had been issued for the schools of that township, some related to order, cleanliness, discipline, and attendance. A few gave directions concerning subjects to be taught and methods to be used.

The Rules specified that "vocal music be taught," that "daily exercises on the blackboard be given in arithmetic," and that special attention be given to "mental arithmetic, the doing of elementary sums in the head; . . . frequent exercises in orthography, performed on slates in classes including all difficult words," also, "the same exercises in geography as the principal points and questions learned by rote, in classes, or singing in concert; . . . original composition shall be required of each scholar, and a similar performance in select speaking; also the elements of drawing, perspective and painting." It was specified that each teacher should hold a public examination and exhibition of his scholars and "to render the performance more entertaining, there shall be additional exercises in speaking and singing by the children. Four Saturdays during the year were set down for each of the ten districts in the townships for these exhibitions.

Since no legislation prescribed a course of study, the plan for education differed widely in various parts of the

State. In a few of the large towns, an effort was made to follow a prescribed course of study with the aid of designated textbooks. But in most of the districts, the teacher prescribed the textbooks which he wished to use and consequently it was extremely difficult to secure any kind of uniformity or grading system as we know it. No doubt one advantage was the opportunity for the bright and industrious pupil to progress rapidly and use textbooks suited to his own stage of advancement. Obviously pupils learned much from their association with older students in the same room and in the reading and recitations which they heard from these older pupils.

By 1857, the teachers institutes were beginning to exert a rather powerful influence in the education of teachers, practically none of whom had had normal school training. In that year, meetings were held in every county under the auspices of the State Teachers Association. They usually lasted for five days and combined practical instruction in the subjects taught, namely: language, arithmetic, penmanship, geography, and vocal music, with general lectures on such subjects as "The relative duties of Teacher and Parent," "The Education of the Senses," "Whispering and its Prevention," "School Houses and Furniture," and "Corporal Punishment."

In his report to the state superintendent, the agent of the Association wrote enthusiastically of the good which was accomplished there, but at the same time he lamented that many teachers did not take advantage of the opportunities offered by the institutes because of indifference, lack of money, opposition to "new-fangled" notions, or weariness in a cause which seemed to be badly rewarded by the people.

It is interesting to contrast these early meetings with those held by the New Jersey Education Association slightly more than one hundred years later in 1962. The meeting in Atlantic City of that year was called by the Association the largest convention of teachers in the world. It lasted for three days, was attended by approximately twenty-eight thousand persons: teachers, administrators, school board members, and other interested people. Its program listed three general meetings, one or more meetings for 28 affiliated groups representing different subject areas of school work, meetings of 11 associations of school workers, such as principals, superintendents, and college faculty members, and meetings of 14 other independent groups connected with educational activities. There were exhibits of books, educational materials, equipment, and many other items related to the operation of schools, by 350 companies, colleges, publishers, and educational organizations. On the last afternoon, as in many previous years, a concert was given by the All-State Chorus and Orchestra, consisting of about 400 high school pupils in the chorus and 135 in the orchestra. The members of the Association in 1862 would have been astonished had they been told that a hundred years later the Association would be erecting an office building in Trenton costing nearly one and a third million dollars.

Most of the school work in the 1860's was routine. Attention to individual differences and to what we think of as encouragement of creativity was absent. The State reports of these years, however, indicate that people were beginning to think that education was more than memorizing facts and that the pupil's interests might well be considered.

In 1862, the meeting of the State Teachers Association considered the report of a Committee on the Course of Study suited to the Public Schools. The Principal of the Trenton Normal School, William Phelps, reported that only one state (Massachusetts) prescribed a course of study. The report elaborated the thought that a "true education embraces all phases that can effect the full and harmonious development of all of the powers of the pupil, the physical, intellectual and moral." New ideas were beginning to be discussed. For example, one finds in the reports of some of the town superintendents mention of "object" teaching and demonstrations of the same by persons from the normal school. This theory of using actual materials in the classroom sprang from the ideas which Pestalozzi had fostered in Europe.

In his report for 1863, the state superintendent spoke of the desirability of making the ways of knowledge the "ways of pleasantness and paths of peace." But he warned that the mind must be "exercised and buffeted," that words and facts alone will not give ideas. "There is danger," he said, "of cramming the minds of young children with nothing more than words," and he wrote that "object" teaching must be in the hands of skillful teachers or it will become formalized and made "a clumsy process by which to cram the mind with useless words." At any rate, some thought was being given to the curriculum and to methods of teaching, in addition to the multitudinous problems of finance, schoolhouses, and how and where to get teachers.

Methods of discipline were also being questioned and changed. One special item in the Act of 1866 was deemed by the state superintendent as worthy of discussion in his report, and that was the prohibition of corporal punishment. He had had reports from some county superintendents that discipline had improved since the use of the rod had been abolished by this Act. Others felt that disorder and insubordination among pupils had greatly increased. He expressed the belief that corporal punishment should not be inflicted but that probably the act of prohibiting it had come too hastily and that it had been unwise to give teachers in the cities the right to use corporal punishment when it was denied to the teachers in the rural districts. New Jersey was early in taking a step which is today recognized as proper in the conduct of schools.

This debate went on for several years. In the reports to the state superintendent in 1874, several county superintendents discussed the question. C. S. Conkling of Hunterdon County said, "A spirit of restlessness, under the prohibition of the rod of correction, has evinced itself with several of our teachers." Another wrote, "A large number of the teachers aver their inability to preserve order and control pupils unless they are allowed to use the rod. This is a mistake. At first, perhaps from the fact that children are allowed so much liberty—or what is worse license at home, one might be led to regard the problem of discipline as a difficult one." Then he goes on to advocate sending the unruly to reform schools rather than using corporal punishment. His comment about the way children were treated at home reminds us that our own day is not unique in believing that children are not properly disciplined at home.

Curriculum revision and new ideas in educational philosophy were also being reflected in textbooks. New sets of Readers were published with more variety in the material. The *Third Reader* in the Willson series, published by Harper and Brothers in New York in 1866, contaiend 62 pages of "Stories from the Bible" with colored illustrations, then 23 pages of "Moral Lessons." In Part II of about one hundred fifty pages, zoology is covered with many informative stories, poems, and articles about animals of all kinds. Thus the reader became almost a textbook on an aspect of science. The *Fifth Reader* in the same series was a formidable volume of 538 pages covering botany, reptiles, human physiology, fishes, civil architecture, geography, chemistry, geology, and finally ancient history prior to the Christian era. Material from famous authors and poems was alternated with articles concerning the various subjects under consideration.

Without doubt, the most influential series of readers from a literary point of view was the McGuffey Readers which appeared in 1837 and continued to be sold in various revised editions until after 1900. William McGuffey grew up under pioneer conditions in Ohio, aspired to be a minister, and eventually became a college professor. His books were a wonderful collection of stories, poems, orations, and dramatic incidents from the greatest of English and American authors. Many think that much of the American way of thinking at the end of the nineteenth century can be traced to McGuffey. It should be kept in mind that children had very few books and that they read and heard the material in McGuffey over and over again. Reading aloud was the vogue and he, as well as other compilers of school readers, emphasized the techniques of elocution, of pronunciation, and articulation.

Although for several years McGuffey's books were sold mainly in Ohio and other midwestern states, they penetrated into the middle states soon after the Civil War and were used to a large extent for the next thirty or forty years. What makes the opinions and convictions of a people? Certainly the schools are not the only factor. People acquire their modes of thinking from parents, newspapers, contact with other people, speeches of their political leaders, and sermons among other sources. In the earlier days when communication was more difficult than it is now, the schools were a tremendous influence in building the character of a people. Mark Sullivan in his *Our Times* devotes nearly two hundred of his 650 pages in the second volume to the influence of the schools and particularly of the McGuffey Readers. He quotes many famous men as remembering years afterwards the selections they read and heard in school.

Many tributes are similar to one in Hamlin Garland's *Son of the Middle Border*:

> I wish to acknowledge my deep obligation to Professor McGuffey, whoever he may have been, for the dignity and grace of his selections. From the pages of his readers, I learned to know and love the poems of Scott, Byron, Southey, Wordsworth, and a long line of English masters. I got my first taste of Shakespeare from the selected scenes which I read in these books.

McGuffey believed that the people who had had approved social experience should direct the inexperienced into ways of happiness and usefulness and his books were designed to bring about this end. In the books for younger children he used animal stories to teach lessons of kindness, loyalty, and faithfulness. He constantly drew from actual experiences of the pioneer country to get his lessons across. His style was interesting and gauged to various levels of reading. When he reached the Fifth and Sixth Readers, he used the great literary selections of the times, drawing on both English and American authors. He hated a lie and admired courage. Drunkenness, luxury, self-pride were constantly condemned. Love of home and country, respect for the Sabbath, and for law, parents, and the aged were stressed. His books contained the experiences of the noblest of mankind—teachers, spiritual leaders, and prophets. Certainly the pupils of our day, although they read more widely, do not acquire at the same age a taste for the great masterpieces of literature which their great-grandparents attained in the second half of the nineteenth century.

A stimulus to wider reading was provided in 1871, when the Legislature offered school districts twenty dollars from state funds if the district raised a like amount for a school library. Reports over succeeding years show that an increasing use was made of this provision, which remained in effect until 1955 when separate funds were consolidated into general school aid, and districts were urged by the Commissioner of Education to use this increased state aid to provide supplementary materials such as library books.

A remarkable stimulus to education in the State came through participation in the Centennial Exposition of 1876 in Philadelphia. School exhibits from many states and from foreign countries were shown at this celebration of the signing of the Declaration of Independence. The state superintendent asked the county superintendents and teachers to submit all kinds of school materials wihch could be exhibited in Philadelphia. The reports at the end of that year show that although a great amount of work was involved, the response was on the whole hearty. Teachers and pupils received much benefit in preparing their exhibits, and citizens felt great pride in going to Philadelphia to see them. The State Superintendent also asked each county superintendent to compile a history of education for his own county. This stimulated much interviewing of oldest inhabitants and the recording of their recollections of schooldays long ago. One man reported that although he did not visit the schools as much as before, he had compiled a history of the school of that county running to 167 pages.

The state superintendent reported that out of 2810 teachers in the State in 1876, 2690 or 95 per cent contributed work done by their pupils. The exhibit consisted of "drawings, maps, mathematical operations, penmanship, grammatical work, composition, primary work, and all other branches of learning pursued in the schools." There were 438 volumes of bound material, with 14,859 specimens of pupils' work, also 237 specimens of drawings and maps in frames. Rutgers College, Princeton College, and 33 private schools also contributed exhibits. That the state superintendent was proud of the exhibit is shown by his quotation, in his annual report, from an article in the *New York Tribune*: "Among the States that made educational exhibits none shows such a comprehensive collection of school work as New Jersey." A room was prepared at the State House to show the exhibit after the close of the Philadelphia Exhibition in the hope that this would serve as a basis for a museum of school work.

One of the recommendations arising from the Centennial came in 1879 when the teachers' institutes were devoted almost entirely to the subject of industrial drawing. An instructor from Boston, a Professor Putnam, was employed to go to all of the institutes and there the teachers, acting as pupils, were supplied with drawing materials and were given lessons in drawing for the entire day. The state superintendent was enthusiastic about the results, and county superintendents reported continuing interest. One said, "I think it is a fair conclusion from the results already seen, that the Institute work has excited a lasting interest in the subject of drawing; that the subject is one of practical importance, and that it can and is likely to be taught in our public schools."

Somewhat related to industrial drawing was manual training, which was first offered in city schools during the next decade. By the end of the ten years it was being offered in 28 cities and towns. In 1888 the Legislature made manual training compulsory in all schools, responding in this way to the growing industrialization of the State. A proposal to add this branch to the work of the normal school was made, but the Trustees were reluctant as they seemed to think that this smacked of "trade training." They did express approval of this kind of a course if it was organized to promote the "perfect development of the human being" as "training of the hand as well as of the intellect." After the abolition of the separate Board of Trustees in 1890 and the transfer of its functions to the State Board of Education, the latter Board approved the addition of manual training to the curriculum in 1891, but a separate department for this work, later called "Industrial Arts," was not organized until 1915.

In evaluating the Centennial exhibits from foreign countries in 1876 the state superintendent came to these conclusions:

1. More central authority would produce great improvement in the construction of schoolhouses.
2. Much improvement was needed in connection with the equipment of schools in scientific apparatus and other illustrative materials.
3. More attention should be given to art education to bring about greater beauty, originality, and novelty in the arts and manufactures.
4. Music should be given a greater role in the school program.
5. Better collections of museum material in the field of natural history should be encouraged.
6. Teaching should be more localized so that children would have a greater appreciation of the particular region where they lived.

7. Technical education should be encouraged in order that the processes of manufacture and the mysteries of the arts should be taught.

"Let us modify our courses of study to meet the demands of the times," he said. Obviously the schools were thinking beyond the three R's and a little geography and American history, to a course of study which would educate pupils to be successful in a society growing in industrial interests. A concept was also developing of giving boys and girls preparation for citizenship and another of directing their leisure time in profitable ways.

During the next decade, great progress was made in realization of these recommendations. In 1890, the Reverend F. R. Brace, Superintendent of Camden County, in his annual report wrote as follows:

> The last twenty years have seen immense progress in everything connected with education, the subjects taught, the methods adopted, the appliances used. It is almost impossible for those not immediately connected with the work to conceive of the advance made. Twenty years ago, in most of the schools in this county, only the rudiments of the elementary branches were taught, and those often in a very imperfect manner. There was no system of instruction of a well-defined character. Indeed, for the county there was no system at all. Not a county in New Jersey, or elsewhere, so far as I know, unless that county was co-terminous with a city, had any system. It was found that in many schools, English grammar, or anything that made any approach to it, was ignored. Geography had small space allotted to it, and even arithmetic was often thrust into a corner.
>
> Such studies as physiology, natural philosophy, bookkeeping, etc. were unknown, except in a few instances. Now, a well-defined course of study is pursued in every school, and most of the schools teach the branches that were supposed to belong to the academies.

In the reports of the state and local superintendents in the 1890's, there are many references to the addition of new subjects to the curriculum, such as art, music, civics, and "physical culture," as it was called. Courses of study were being constructed in many communities. Superintendent Benjamin C. Gregory of Trenton said that new courses of study were constructed in 1888, 1894, and again in 1899. By 1899, a large number of teachers were involved in the discussions. In his report, Gregory wrote of fitting the course to the psychology of child development, of defining purposes more definitely, of giving specific instruction where needed, of providing for correlation of subjects, of using concrete materials wherever possible, and of utilizing much collateral information outside the regular textbooks.

In 1895, the State Board of Education ordered all county superintendents to prepare and establish uniform courses of study. This ruling stimulated active examination of the material being taught and the preparation of syllabi to guide the teachers. In 1894, a "Free Textbook Act" had been passed providing all books needed at public expense. State Superintendent Addison B. Poland said that this step constituted the "last remaining impediment to making schools absolutely free."

By the end of the century, schools in the cities and large towns were organized so that the children of a single grade were together in one room. In rural areas many one-room schools still existed where children of several grades, sometimes from the first through the eighth, were taught by one teacher. The grading of schools created a condition in which subject matter could be arranged in sequential order and adapted to the average capabilities of children of a given grade. This stimulated constant study by the school staff of what should be taught at each level. Teachers began to share with administrators the construction of courses of study. More attention was being given to defining desirable accomplishments in the newer subjects of the curriculum such as music, art, and manual training. Even in the one-room schools, much help was given to the teacher by the county superintendent in defining goals

This picture of an upper grade in Ridgewood appeared in the State Report of the State Superintendent of Schools in 1899. (The customary rows of desks indicate the formality of the program). The girl at the blackboard is "diagramming" a sentence which was a common exercise in the study of grammar.

and dividing subject matter into units for each age level.

Looking back over the century one can see the progress from a simple curriculum of reading, spelling, writing, and a little arithmetic to a broad offering involving geography, history, elementary science, music, art, and manual training. A beginning had been made toward the constant re-study of the curriculum to bring it into greater social usefulness and to adjust it to the needs of the many kinds of children in the schools. A foundation had been constructed for the more intensive work in revision which began with the twentieth century.

VI

THE TWENTIETH CENTURY—THE SCIENTIFIC REVOLUTION

When America turned into the twentieth century, it had just emerged from its baptism in international conflict. The war with Spain over Cuba was not a major one, but it threw upon us the guardianship of the Philippines in Asia and opened up a road which has constantly led to more and more involvement in world affairs. Who in 1900 could have predicted that in the next half-century we would become engaged in two world conflicts and become the donors of billions of dollars in aid to underdeveloped countries throughout the world? Who could have predicted that in spite of these wars and a major depression, the country in the 1960's would be in the midst of general prosperity far above that enjoyed by the masses of people in 1900?

At the opening of the twentieth century, people knew nothing of airplanes, radio or television, or man-made satellites circling the earth. Anyone who had predicted these phenomena would have been thought an impractical visionary or a madman. A few eccentrics were driving around in "horseless carriages" making themselves something of a nuisance to people driving horses. The telephone was still a rarity. Homes were usually lighted by kerosene lamps or by gas. Thomas Edison was still tinkering with electrical experiments. Roads, except in the cities where main streets were paved with cobblestones, were of dirt. Hundreds of devices now used in ordinary homes were unknown. The following period of scientific revolution lay beyond the imagination of anyone living in 1900.

The worker of that time was getting between $1.50 and $2.00 per day instead of an average of $2.40 per *hour* for factory workers and between $3.50 and $5.00 per *hour* for the skilled worker at the present time. The average wage of all workers on railroads in that year was $11.43 per week and the average earnings of workers in all industries, excluding farmers, was $490 per year. In 1957, this average was $4211. Although no accurate figures exist for a comparison of the present purchasing value of the dollar with that of 1900, the Research Division of the National Education Association has computed from government figures, the 1912-dollar as worth three of today's dollars. A rough estimate would indicate that one dollar in 1900 was worth four dollars in purchasing power in 1963. Taking account of this difference it can be said that the industrial worker of today is receiving at least twice as much as he did in 1900. Furthemore, men worked from fifty to sixty hours per week in 1900 instead of thirty-five to forty.

The average salary of male teachers was $86.21 per month and that of female teachers $48.12, whereas in 1962 the average was $640 per month without distinction in sex. Here, too, the salary has just about doubled in real value.

Henry Ford shocked the business world in 1914 when he proposed paying $5.00 per day for workers in his automobile factory. He was among the first to understand that mass production by means of the assembly line required prosperity in order that the products of highly efficient industry could be purchased. If there is to be mass prosperity, there must be a high level of technical skill and of general education in order that goods may be produced and purchased by the population. The ideal of education for all the children has kept parallel with this technological revolution in industry and commerce.

This has meant more than the extension of education to the high school and to the college. It has had a significant effect on the elementary school, the universal school of a democracy. Unlike the school of Europe, the elementary school is not the school for all for a relatively short period of about five years, after which those who can afford it or are of a certain social class go onto secondary education and the university. In America, the elementary school must lay the groundwork for all, with the supposition that a large percentage of the pupils will go to high school and a considerable number, perhaps 30 per cent or 40 per cent, will go to college. And it must prepare all for participation in the astounding society of the sixties and the next decades, which are going to see even faster changes.

In 1900 great expansion was occurring in oil, railroads, steel, and many similar industries. The increase in opportunities for work brought thousands of new citizens to America, not only from the countries of northern Europe whence earlier groups had immigrated, but also from countries of southeastern Europe, where people had not known the kind of democratic life they found here.

In 1920 there were about fourteen million foreign-born people in the United States, of whom 48.6 per cent came from northern European stock and 50.1 per cent from southern European stock. In the city of Trenton in 1920, of a population of 119,289, 30,073 or 25.2 per cent were foreign born.

Under these conditions, a new language had to be learned and new customs assimilated. The elementary school was, of all our institutions, the "melting pot" for our new citizens. It became much more than a place where fundamental instruction took place. It became an agency for the development of knowledge, skills, attitudes, and aesthetic appreciation needed for full participation in American life.

Even though the school buildings of 1900 were far in advance of those of earlier eras, they would be considered entirely inadequate by present-day standards of well-lighted classrooms, movable furniture, gymnasiums, libraries, medical rooms, lunchrooms, and auditoriums. In 1900, the population of the State was 1,883,669 and the total enrollment in the schools about 336,000, with an average attendance of 221,000. Only about 15,000 were reported as being enrolled in "high school," so that the school problem was mainly an elementary one. In 1960, the population was 6,066,782 and the enrollment in 1962-63 will reach 1,160,000 with approximately 840,000 children in elementary schools and grades 7 and 8 of junior high schools.

Even though 443 new elementary buildings have been erected in the ten years between 1952 and 1962 at a cost of $206,000,000 dollars, there are 47,000 pupils on half-session, and it is estimated that 4000 classrooms are needed within the next year or two to take care of this deficiency and growth in enrollment.

For a picture of the total elementary school enrollment in the State, there must be added to the numbers given above those enrolled in the Catholic schools. No figures are available for those enrolled in other private schools, but in proportion to the total this number is so small as to be negligible.

The first distinctly parochial Catholic school in the State for which there is any record was established in St. John's Parish in Newark in 1833 by Father Patrick Moran. The school was closed in 1925 due to industrial development in the area. The first such school to have continuous existence to the present day was established by Father Bernard McQuade in St. Vincent's Parish in Madison in 1847. Several schools were established in the 1850's and the number grew rapidly during the second half of the nineteenth century, so that by 1900 a majority of parishes had their own elementary schools.

Since 1900 there has been steady growth, so that at the present time there are approximately 253,000 children in 458 Catholic elementary schools with a total faculty of

5574. Thus it can be seen that these schools are making a very sizable contribution to the State's total educational effort.

As they contemplated the changes being brought about by rapid technological and industrial advances, what were the school officials of 1900 thinking about? What emphases were uppermost? The State Superintendent of Schools started his report for the year ending in June 1901 as follows:

> The first year of the new century finds New Jersey ably maintaining her educational rank among the sisterhood of states. Our most liberal, intelligent, and progressive citizens were never so interested in the public schools, never so deeply impressed with their importance to the Commonwealth, and never so helpful in the effort to establish a correct educational sentiment throughout the State. A higher standard of qualification and better salaries for our teachers, more thorough and effective instruction, more advanced and rational courses of study, and more adequate sanitary school accommodations are the demands of the times, and to these the people are ably and generously responding. Progress is the watchword.

Legislation making kindergarten an integral part of the public school system was passed in March, 1900. Even though only a few municipalities took advantage of the law at once, there was in 1900-1901 a reported enrollment of 15,066. The state superintendent endorsed the kindergarten because, as he said, in it "the spontaneity and joy of play is gradually and skillfully brought to bear upon work and the child thus early and unconsciously is made aware that enthusiasm lightens labor."

Extensive reports about school libraries indicated that over twelve thousand dollars had been spent in that year, as the State matched the money spent by each district. The superintendent urged greater expenditure as he said:

> . . . the desire and ability to investigate a subject thoroughly and intelligently is one of the most valuable results of correct

training and instruction in school, and one that will lead to larger and richer growth in after years.

He also reported a decrease in the number of private schools which, he admitted, provided special kinds of opportunities not practicable in the curriculum of the smaller public schools, but he urged the more liberal support of the common school which "should be so well equipped, its instruction so excellent, its moral tone so pronounced, and its environment so attractive that no child, save for exceptional reasons, will be sent elsewhere." It is of interest to note that, even with a decrease of 63 in that year, there were 148 non-sectarian and 155 sectarian private schools, enrolling over 25 pupils each.

The reports of the county and the city superintendents showed there had been a considerable increase in attention to music, art, manual training, and physical education. One man wrote at length against "fads in education" and opposed "silly and experimental methods during the foundation period of any child's life," and many reported on the difficult examinations which were obligatory for a diploma from grammar school. Medical inspection is referred to by several, as well as a determined effort to enforce the compulsory attendance law.

That education of the handicapped was well under way is indicated by the report of the State School for the Deaf, showing an enrollment of 139 children from 20 counties. Its superintendent reported that a good common school education was their aim, with the addition of woodworking, printing, sewing, and shoemaking for the older pupils.

People were also beginning to realize that large classes were not conducive to efficient teaching or attention to the needs of individuals. The average number of pupils per class for 1900-1901 was 44, which was two less than in the preceding year. The state superintendent urged that this be brought down to 40 and, in time, to 30. In 1962 the median was 26, and most school systems aimed at between 25 and 30 in an elementary classroom.

Just as science began to transform society in the early years of the twentieth century, so education began to talk of itself as a "science" as well as an "art." In the first decade of the century, graduate work in education developed in Teachers College, Columbia University, and soon other universities organized departments or "schools" of education. In the sixties, practically every unversity in the nation has such a department, and many teachers colleges have grown to be state colleges with graduate departments. Studies were being made in the psychology of learning and the subjects of the curriculum. Studies in psychology led to an understanding of child growth and development, which is required today of every elementary teacher. Studies in the curriculum delved into the realistic needs of children in the world they would enter, and revolutionized the content of readers, arithmetic, geography, history, and science texts.

The object of such studies was to find out what was really needed in life and to construct a course of study which could meet these needs and not "train the mind" on puzzles or material of little value. Application to real life was made the objective rather than memorizing isolated facts.

This approach to education was soon to be expressed in the measurement of a child's intelligence. Following the work of Alfred Binet and Théodore Simon in France relating especially to below-normal children, work was undertaken in this country by Edward Lee Thorndike and others to develop group tests which could be evaluated from the responses on paper to words, arithmetic problems, and other items. So there developed the concept of the "Intelligence Quotient" which indicated the relationship of a child to children of his own age. An intelligence quotient of 100 meant that a child had average intelligence, whereas a score above this indicated a degree of intelligence above average and one below 100 similar degrees below the average. Children of above-average ability could be identified and challenged to do better work and children of below-average ability could be helped to work within their particular capabilities. Children could be classified into groups in accordance with their intellectual ability.

Techniques of intelligence testing have been improved, and it has been recognized that environment and educational opportunities have a decided effect on the responses given to the items used in testing. An I. Q. is not now considered such a fixed attribute as it once was. It has also been recognized that at present no tests are available which can predict with any degree of accuracy a child's potential or his future contribution to society. Current researches into "creativity" indicate that the traditional intelligence tests tend to measure only a few of the many dimensions of the mind. If teachers are aware of these limitations, intelligence tests are of great value in assisting the teacher in challenging a child to reach his greatest possible accomplishments.

Later came a great number of achievement tests in practically every subject of the curriculum, and testing bureaus grew in number in universities and independently. Now schools use, as a matter of course, a large battery of standardized tests by which they can classify pupils according to their relationship to standard grade-norms secured from thousands of pupils. This is a very valuable measure of accomplishment. One danger in these tests has been that in order to get answers which can be corrected objectively, they have tended to emphasize factual knowledge which can be put down in a blank, or marked "True" or "False," or selected from a group of answers provided answer. Achievement tests of the pencil-and-paper variety can measure only a limited kind of learning. They cannot to any appreciable degree measure thinking, creating, and valuing. When overemphasized, achievement testing tends to narrow the curriculum to the elements which can be measured by the test. Good schools in New Jersey recognize these limitations and use these tests as only one method of measuring accomplishment.

Meanwhile, John Dewey was working on and writing about his philosophy of education which was based on the theory that education ought to improve living. So many interpretations have been given to his philosophy and its effects on the schools that it is difficult to arrive at its true meaning and accomplishment. In the beginning at least, it was certainly concerned with broadening the concept of education to include the relationship of the social environment to the life of the pupil. It called for the application of the new research to the fields of psychology and the social sciences. Dewey acknowledged the problem of educating "all the children of all the people" and advocated practices which would fit all kinds of children and prepare them for actual life in a democracy.

A difficulty arose, however, when a corps of disciples misrepresented, in many ways, the fundamental theories which Dewey enunciated. Thus, there developed the "project method," which was based on activities suggested by the children and presumed to be of vital interest to them in current living. The term "child-centered" school was opposed to the "subject-centered" school, and those who would prescribe a set course of study were brought into ridicule. It was the basis for the formation of a society known as the "Progressive Education Association" which lasted from 1919 to 1955. During its existence it had a multitude of followers and many enemies, and it stimulated wide discussion of the American educational program. The Association did advance American education by establishing the importance of teaching children the methods of discovery. Some think it declined as a vital force because it could not free itself from its absorption with the individual and come to grips with the ever-changing problems of an industrialized democracy. Certainly not all of the criticisms which are now thrown at education can be blamed on "progressive" education. Many other forces in society will have to be analyzed to understand why the school does not always succeed in bringing the pupils to expected accomplishments, or why particular steps are advocated.

Freeing the child from old restraints was important, however. In the twenties, screwed-to-the-floor desks and chairs gave way to movable tables and chairs, thus making it much easier to teach groups instead of the whole class and to adjust the program to individual differences. The relationship between teacher and pupil became more informal and more friendly. One of the first things noticed by visitors from European schools is this friendly relationship. More creative work has been introduced, especially in art, and children are encouraged to express their ideas in their own personal manner. Physical education began to utilize more games and fewer formal exercises. The study of dramatics was promoted and children were encouraged to develop originality in getting their ideas across to their mates and their parents. Elocution has given way to playing a role in a simple dramatic episode.

Recently, the difficulty which some children have in learning to read has been attributed to the influence of "progressive" education. Just what connection exists is hard to identify. It is true that as "progressive education" developed, a change came about in the teaching of reading. In the late nineteenth century it had been recognized that the alphabet method of teaching reading was defective. Teaching of sounds by the "phonetic" method was adopted and children were also taught to associate vowels with consonants in families, as had been done in the early Webster *Speller*. But there came to be such an emphasis on marking vowels with diacritical marks that they were hardly recognizable. Then came the era of teaching entire words and sometimes even sentences without regard to sounds of the letters or their markings. The better pupils learned to read, but poorer pupils had great difficulty and lacked a means of helping themselves as they had no way of understanding the sounds of letters, especially vowels. The dictionary was unintelligible for pronunciation as the marks on the vowels meant nothing, and spelling was much more difficult.

Reading is now recognized as the most fundamental school subject, which must be mastered if other subjects are to be learned well. Oral reading of the old style of one hundred years ago has gone out, and effort is directed toward the kind of mastery which will enable him to understand the meaning of what he reads. "Why can't Johnny read?" is the cry of those who favor a more formalized school program. It is difficult to get evidence as to comparative ability of the present-day pupil with the one of fifty or seventy-five years ago. There seems to be some evidence that today's child does better on the fundamentals than yesterday's did. But criticism has led the schools to re-examine their programs, and to bring back those elements of an earlier program which may have been discarded too hastily. Remedial techniques in reading, which have been proven by scientific experiments, are now being used and the phonetic elements of reading are recognized as having a proper place in the total program.

Adapting the schools to the problems of the twentieth century has been brought about not only by changes in philosophy, testing procedures, curriculum revisions, and methods of teaching but also by improvements in administration. These have had a direct effect on advances made. Certain changes were made in the State administration of schools which, with minor modifications, have remained in operation ever since and have provided a commendable stability. In 1910, as the result of the recommendations of a State survey (the Frelinghuysen Commission), the office of State Superintendent of Schools was abolished and a Commissioner of Education appointed, with a staff of assistant commissioners and directors, with powers and duties far beyond previous conceptions of this office. The commissioner is appointed by the governor for a term of five years and works under the authority of a State Board of Education. At first, this was an eight-member board, but it was enlarged to ten in 1921 and to twelve in 1945. It has been composed of eminent citizens and has never been involved in political considerations. The commissioner's office has been greatly enlarged so that leadership is provided in every phase of educational work from the kindergarten through the university.

New Jersey has always delegated much authority to local school districts. Standards of teacher certification, school buildings, accounting, transportation of pupils, high school requirements, and certain other legal provisions are administered by the State office, but within the legal requirements and certain rules established by the State Board of Education, local districts have complete authority to set up courses of study, select textbooks, hire teachers, and perform many other functions of school operation. As a matter of fact, legislation has never prescribed subjects for elementary schools, and no examinations are given by State authorities. For several years, eighth grade examinations were required, but this law was repealed in 1928, as it was felt that local authorities could exercise better judgment in the matter of promoting pupils than could be accomplished by statewide examinations.

The abolition of school districts and the establishment of the township system in 1894 gave the State a sound system of school administration. Cities and large towns and boroughs have professional superintendents of schools, and the rural communities without such officers get professional supervision from the county superintendent of schools. School boards are usually composed of nine members, either appointed by the mayor in cities or elected by the people in the townships and boroughs. A few cities elect the members of the school board. Consolidation of schools, which has been made possible by good roads and efficient transportation, makes it possible to have large schools with non-teaching principals who can give some time to actual supervision of instruction. In 1961, it was reported that 289,642 pupils were transported in 4500 vehicles at a cost of nearly fifteen million dollars. Thus the small elementary school with its inadequate building, poorly prepared teacher, and outworn textbooks has practically disappeared.

One of the most far-reaching projects for aiding the rural and small schools in the early part of the century was the inauguration of the "helping teacher" system in 1916. It was first initiated through the generosity of an interested citizen who contributed money for the experiment. The theory behind this proposal was that an experienced teacher be employed to aid the teachers in the small schools, who had not had standard training. It was really a normal school on the job. The helping teacher gave demonstration lessons, assisted the teacher with children who needed special help, recommended textbooks, suggested new methods of teaching, and performed many other functions to aid the inexperienced teacher. She was employed by the State but assigned to a given county. So successful was the initial experiment that it was extended to other counties, and by the mid-twenties there were about thirty-five such people employed under the direction of the county superintendents and the assistant commissioner in charge of elementary education. As of 1963, there are 60 "Helping Teacher" positions authorized and twelve "Supervisors of Child Study" located in 19 of the 21 counties. Their functions have changed somewhat as schools have become consolidated and standards for beginning teachers have improved. But, inasmuch as not enough teachers can be found with standard certification, those with less than this preparation tend to be employed in the rural and small-town districts, and they need much assistance to enable them to meet the requirements of present-day society in the elementary school. They give to these schools the kind of supervision which in a city comes from the principal and the supervisors who work from the office of the superintendent of schools.

A new feature in the organization of schools, which has had a permanent effect on elementary education, was the growth of the junior high school which began in the early years of the century and has continued. Combining Grades 7 and 8 from the elementary school with Grade 9 of the high school had certain advantages. It was felt that in the traditional organization there had been a tendency to continue stereotypes of the earlier grades not well adapted to the developing interests and abilities of the adolescent. The "teen-age" child needed more choice than was afforded, and was looking forward to differentiation in accordance with future interests.

The erection of new buildings for junior high schools gave opportunity to provide for a much wider curriculum, for gymnasiums, for departmentalization of teaching, and for better orientation of the work in line with the objectives and demands of the secondary school. With the growing population, the building of junior high schools or sometimes of a six-year school composed of Grades 7 through 12, has relieved the crowded elementary schools and has created a new type of school organization. Naturally, this kind of school has spread more rapidly in cities than in the more rural areas, but the building of consolidated and regional schools has fostered its growth there, too. In 1963, approximately 42 per cent of the pupils in Grades 7 and 8 are in junior high schools or six-year schools for Grades 7 to 12.

The scientific attitude towards education resulted in a re-examination of the entire curriculum and a remarkable amount of activity, especially in the twenties, in construction of courses of study. In 1918, the Commission on the Reorganization of Secondary Education issued the famous seven "Cardinal Principles," of which the first six were also pertinent to elementary education. These seven principles were as follows: health, command of the fundamental processes, worthy home membership, civic education, worthy use of leisure time, development of ethical character, and vocational education. Many other students of education issued similar lists, similar in nature but with different emphases. The State Department of Education organized committees from many communities representing different fields of the elementary school curriculum. As a result of their work, it published several monographs covering practically all of the subjects taught. Although cities and larger communities published their own courses of study, it was estimated by the Commission to Survey Public Education in 1928 that the State courses were used in approximately 57 per cent of all school districts, and by 78 per cent of districts of less than five thousand in population.

Many cities and large township districts formulated new courses of study through local committees aided by experts from universities and the teacher training institutions. Thus, enthusiastic interest was engendered in a re-examination of the elementary school program and its relationship to children of various abilities. The courses were usually organized around four major headings: objectives, subject matter to be taught, methods to be used, and bibliography and aids for effective teaching. The construction of such courses did much to bring teachers into the foreground as primary forces not only in classroom work but also in the formulation of plans and programs of instruction. In recent years, the Elementary Division of the State Department of Education has helped the county and local teachers in their curriculum revision program with curriculum guides and consultant services.

One of the influences of "progressive" education was to stimulate the use of "units of work" in the organization of the elementary curriculum rather than following sequential descriptions of subject matter laid out for each grade. The skillful teacher in organizing a "unit" would bring together material from several fields and thus, by correlating them, show how these various items were related in the problem under discussion. One difficulty has been that other teachers of succeeding grades would not know what had been covered. The result was the lack of a complete plan to be followed during the entire life of the child in the elementary school. At the present time, there seems to be a tendency to return to a more sequential organization of subject matter, while at the same time keeping some of the values of the correlated unit.

The State's concern for the education of retarded children was expressed in 1911 in a law mandating special education for children three or more years below the normal. Over the years much progress was made in testing, classifying, and teaching such children. In 1954, new legislation was passed requiring education for the mentally retarded and physically handicapped. Since then, classes have been organized for the "educables," the higher level of ability among the retarded, and those of a lower level, the "trainables." At present, "Special Education Services" in the State include services of teachers working with more than 13,000 retarded children. The teachers of more than 175 classes serve almost 1500 physically handicapped children. Approximately 750 teachers provide individual instruction at home for about 2500 children. About 300 teachers give special instruction to 7000 partially-sighted, blind, speech-defective, and crippled children who are able to attend classes in schools but need supplemental instruction.

The State's concern for deaf children has been shown in the new school opened in West Trenton in 1923, taking the place of the one established in 1883. This school is on a beautiful site of 116 acres on which have been erected buildings valued at six and a half million dollars. In 1963, there were 425 pupils in the school, from four to twenty-one years of age, divided into three units: the nursery, the lower, middle and upper schools. There are 78 people on the professional staff.

There has been no development, however, in education of children below the kindergarten level at public expense. Many nursery schools are conducted under private auspices. In fact, in 1962, 348 such schools were licensed by the State Department of Education as meeting proper standards. A relatively small number of children are in these schools.

A major change occurred in the organization of schools when the law forbidding discrimination "against persons because of race, creed, color, national origin or ancestry" was passed in 1945. Up to that time, segregated elementary schools for Negroes existed southward from a line drawn across the State, approximately from Princeton to Asbury Park. In communities south of that line, separate facilities were maintained, although a few Negroes attended other schools when they lived too far to walk to the Negro school. It was not acceptable, however, to have Negro teachers in white schools. The 1945 law set up in the State Department of Education a Division against Discrimination, now called the Division on Civil Rights, to handle disputes under the law and to encourage integration. Results of this law were excellent; integration took place without difficulty of any moment; and Negro teachers have been employed in schools used mainly by whites.

At present, another problem has arisen because of the fact that when the boundaries of a school district serving elementary school children are the neighborhood from which the children can walk to school and go home for lunch, a majority of pupils in certain districts may happen to be Negroes. Although originating in living and housing conditions, this becomes a school concern when groups believe that unequal educational opportunities exist. In junior and senior high schools which serve larger districts with a more heterogeneous population, the problem is not so acute, but in the elementary district it is a serious one, the solution of which is not yet apparent. It must be the object of a school system to provide adequate facilities and educational opportunities for all children in accordance with their educational needs, and this seems to be the aim of the school system in New Jersey. The schools are seriously concerned to give the "culturally deprived" child the experiences which will help him to find his way to successful living in American society.

How is the modern elementary school meeting the problem of educating all of the children of all the people? How does it strive to give a fundamental education and also to stimulate those who have high capacity to make the best use of their talents, and to bring to the greatest possible achievement the abilities of those of lesser capacity?

Although he may be difficult to find, let us suppose that there is an individual now living in our State who has not been in an elementary school since his childhood days of fifty years ago. We observe his impressions and reactions as we visit with him one of the approximately four hundred new elementary schools which have been built in New Jersey from 1953 through 1962.

As we approach the building, we become immediately aware of the revolution in school design which began around 1950 and will continue for some years to come. The "little red schoolhouse" of the rural countryside and the multi-storied city school with its rectangular classrooms arranged in "train-type" fashion along dark, narrow, locker-lined, high-ceilinged corridors, have both almost disappeared from the New Jersey scene. The building we are about to enter may be a campus school, a "cluster school," a finger-type building, a "school in the round," or any of the other newer designs which represent a sharp break with the traditional school building of yesteryear.

As we enter the building, we are amazed at the light, airy, pleasant, attractive, and spacious interior. Our friend remarks that it is far different from the gloomy, unattractive, and vaguely depressing building he remembers so well from his own school days. Gone are the "battleship grays" and "schoolhouse browns" which used to cover every wall and floor. Our modern school has a light, durable, easy-to-clean, and attractive floor covering which easily absorbs the sound of busy feet. The inside walls are painted or tiled in soft pastel colors, soft rose or pale yellow for northern exposures and cool blue, sea green, or pale violet for southern exposures.

As we make a quick tour of the building, we point out the rooms and facilities entirely strange to our friend. We pass through the all-purpose room which serves as a

Public School No. 3 in Fairview is typical of elementary school buildings in the late nineteenth and early twentieth centuries. It is a box-like structure containing practically nothing but classrooms.

cafeteria, playroom, or small theater, as the need arises. Here is the medical-dental suite. The school nurse points out such facilities as equipment for testing vision and hearing, scales and charts to measure growth and development, equipment for dental examinations, first-aid supplies, a file of complete medical records on all pupils, and the separate cubicles used for emergency care or physical examinations.

Our next stop is the school library, which is one of the most important and frequently-used areas. The book-filled shelves beckon invitingly to readers of various ages. The comfortable furniture provides a pleasant place to browse or study. The card catalogue, encyclopedias, atlases, almanacs, and numerous reference books help to provide children with the information and study skills they will need in high school and college.

Even in 1934, there were only three elementary school libraries as such. In 1959, there were only 35 elementary

The Vanderveer School in Somerville is a common type of postwar school. The one-story wings provide easy access to every room. The gymnasium and other activity rooms provide opportunity for a rich program for all children.

school librarians, whereas in the fall of 1961 there were 145 such librarians working either in a single school or sometimes serving in as many as ten. The modern school would not think of omitting this adjunct to a child's education.

We move on across the hall to visit the instructional materials center. Here are kept the tape recorders, record players, film-strip projectors, overhead projectors, opaque projectors, flannel or magnetic boards, materials for producing learning aids, files of transparencies, mounted pictures, slides, and filmstrips, and all of the other equipment and resources which the modern elementary teacher uses to clarify, enrich, and supplement his teachings.

Down the hall, we pass offices of the principal, various curricula specialists (reading, science, art, music, etc.), the school psychologist, and the guidance worker. In answer to a questioning look from our friend, we explain that the modern elementary school is concerned not only with the academic growth of the pupil, but with his social, physical, and emotional development as well. This broadened concept of education necessitates an interdisciplinary approach, in which the classroom teacher is a member of a "team," along with the psychologist, school physician, administrator, guidance worker, school social worker, and many others: a team which provides guidance for each individual pupil according to his needs.

Now we enter a classroom which happens to be the fourth grade. As we enter the room, our friend gasps in amazement. Where are the rows of desks and chairs fastened to the floor? Where are the long-remembered slate boards and dusty erasers of another era? Where is the death-like quiet which used to reign in every "good" teacher's classroom? First of all, the stationary rows of furniture have been replaced by movable furniture which makes the room adaptable for the wide variety of ac-

This view of a kindergarten room in a modern school shows not only the kind of lighting and furniture provided, but also how the teacher can work with a group while other children are occupied in varied activities.

This third grade classroom in a modern school shows the kind of furniture, blackboard, bulletin boards and other equipment now furnished. In this kind of setting, the teacher can work with individuals or groups while others are engaged in different kinds of learning activities.

tivities found in a broad educational program. The furniture is lightweight, compact, easy to move and store, the working surfaces covered with a durable plastic finish. (No initials can be carved into *these* desks!) There are some individual desks and chairs, but much of the furniture consists of tables of various shapes (square, trapezoidal, semi-circular, oval, S-shaped), which can be easily grouped into a variety of seating arrangements according to pupil activities.

Look at the children now. They are doing so many different things, it is difficult to determine exactly what "lesson" is being taught. Sitting around the teacher in one corner are about a dozen children reading from their literature text and discussing what they are reading. We realize that the teacher is working with a group on about the same level of accomplishment, and that other groups may be given quite a different exercise.

The rest of the class is engaged in a great variety of activities. Some are working at their desks. Three boys are tracing an outline map projected by an opaque projector on a huge sheet of brown wrapping paper. Two others are poring over an atlas. One child is painting at an easel. Another is working on a science project. Yet, as these children work at so many different tasks, we notice no confusion or unnecessary noise. Nor, as our friend remarks, do any of the children seem as bored as he remembers being when he went to school. On the contrary, as we watch teacher and pupils working together, we sense that these children are actually excited about learning. They are eagerly seeking answers and exploring new areas of knowledge. They are working at their own rates of speed according to their own abilities. Their wise teacher recognizes the differences in experiential background, mental ability, motivation, and interest which exist among these pupils (even though they are all at the same grade level) and she develops her daily program accordingly.

A noticeable feature of the new elementary classroom is the increased use of tackboards or bulletin boards. In other classrooms, reversible chalk-board units, or portable boards, sliding boards, boards on folding panels, or free-standing room dividers are surfaced so that they can be used for display purposes.

Of all the many innovations he has noticed, our friend is most enthusiastic about the abundance and variety of learning aids. Who could be bored or resistant toward learning with all these materials within easy reach? In one section of the room, for instance, is the library nook. It contains a small reading table, a few comfortable chairs, and skillfully arranged bookcases, shelves, and space dividers. In this corner are kept supplementary books, periodicals, an encyclopedia, dictionaries, maps, globes, atlases, newspapers, and other reading aids which children use constantly.

Another popular area is the art corner. This contains a large, flat-surfaced table, an easel, a drying rack for the children's paintings, and adequate storage space for their work. Neatly stored are various art supplies including paints, crayons, brushes, chalk, drawing boards, paint tins, paste, clay, plasticene, bits of colored glass, tile, and seeds for making mosaics, weaving looms and materials, block-printing equipment, and other aids to the development of the creative talents of each pupil.

Every elementary classroom today has a science center, and this room is no exception. It contains, at various times of the year, collections of leaves, fossils, insects, shells, etc. Scientific books and periodicals are a permanent part of the center. In addition, there are various types of living things: goldfish, tropical fish, turtles, chickens, frogs, toads, snakes, tadpoles, rabbits. These offer children valuable learning experiences. Experimental equipment, records of data, and other materials necessary to implement a vital science program are also carefully kept in the science center.

Throughout the year, other "centers of interest" are created in the room as the need arises. The children tell us, for instance, of their music center, hobby center, arithmetic corner, and creative writing nook, all of which they have used from time to time.

As we leave the building, we attempt to summarize the outstanding features of the modern elementary school we have noticed on this very short visit. In brief, they seem to be: (1) a broad educational program aimed at the optimum physical, mental, social and emotional development of each individual, (2) a healthful and pleasant physical environment, (3) a stimulating intellectual environment in every classroom, (4) an abundance and variety of multi-sensory learning aids, (5) a positive social environment in which children work and play in harmony and with respect for others, (6) respect for the unique abilities of each individual, (7) a well-educated, competent staff-team of classroom teachers and specialized personnel, and (8) emphasis upon the skills of creative thinking and independent intellectual inquiry.

The elementary school, like the other divisions of the school system, can meet its problems efficiently only if properly financed. In 1871, the citizens thought they had solved this problem by passing the two-mill tax on property, to be levied by the State. Soon, townships had to add money from their own taxes. Several years later, this tax was increased to two and three-quarters mills, and railroads were taxed for the benefit of the schools. But as population grew and school services expanded, these amounts declined in proportion to the total needed. Taxes on the property of citizens grew enormously.

Finally, in 1947, the State abandoned the property tax and the railroad tax as taxes dedicated to school purposes. It also put the income of the State School Fund, the principal of which had grown to over $14,000,000 with an annual income of $450,000, into the general treasury as part of the total amount distributed by the State to aid education in the local communities. This amount from the State has grown to approximately $100,000,000, but in 1963 was only about 24 per cent of the total local expense, whereas the average in the entire United States is 40 per cent. In the neighboring states of New York and Pennsylvania, the state contributes 43 per cent and 45 per cent respectively. The Tax Commission in its 1963 report has recommended large increases in state aid, changes in the distribution, and other changes to assist the local districts. These new sums will have to come from some new form of tax such as sales or income as in most other states. New Jersey is a wealthy state, as is evidenced by its expenditure of nearly $475 per pupil in 1962, but a limit seems to have been reached in money available from property taxation. It would appear that educational advancement can come only through increased assistance from the State.

What are the problems of the immediate future in improving the elementary school? The main one is to secure more funds from the State so that the separate communities can provide the kind of education required in our times. There is still a dangerous gap between classrooms available and the number needed. To secure a sufficient supply of teachers with standard preparation is a continuing problem. In the area of teaching, more must be done to bring classroom teaching up to the level of what research and knowledge have made available. Expert supervision is required to help teachers make use of current knowledge. New visual and auditory aids must be provided. In a rapidly developing world, teachers must be constantly improving their intellectual equipment. They must be able to adapt to the new social environments of their pupils and new kinds of organization to fit those needs. For example, it is possible that one teacher to one classroom is not the most efficient method of teaching.

This does not mean that elementary schools should adopt the kind of departmental teaching which is used in junior high schools and high schools. Some experimentation has taken place in what is called "team teaching" in which a group of teachers handles a large number of children according to the needs of the children and the special abilities of the teachers to meet these needs. One teacher might be a reading specialist, another a science specialist, and so on. The idea offers rich possibilities for giving to each child and to reasonably homogeneous groups of children the kinds of guidance and teaching designed to promote their greatest possible development. To be an expert in all of the areas of knowledge now being taught is becoming more and more difficult, so that teacher specialization may be one way to improve the school's efficiency, provided all of the teachers in a given school are working under a coordinated plan which utilizes their separate abilities to achieve an integrated result.

Ask children why they like their schools or dislike them, and invariably the first answer will be the teacher. Ahead of the equipment or the auditorium or the gymnasium or particular programs will be the influence of the person who directs these activities. It is this person who stimulates them to love or to detest the intellectual, physical, and social opportunities which the school offers. The original education and continuing growth of this person become of prime importance in the development of good schools.

VII

TEACHER EDUCATION FOR A NEW AGE

At the close of the nineteenth century, one State normal school existed, the one at Trenton established in 1855. It had grown from the 15 students who entered in that year to an enrollment of 565 with 191 graduates in 1900.

For a time the original two-year course had been modified by adding another year for students who came without adequate preparation for the work required. But, as high schools grew in number so that nearly all students had acceptable preparation, the school reverted to a two-year course in 1911. From 1899 to 1917 a program of four years was offered to train high school teachers but as this was taken by only a few students, the school returned to its prime function of training elementary teachers, until a later date when it became a teachers college and other curricula were added.

A kindergarten course was opened in 1899, and in 1901 this was organized as a separate curriculum, thus meeting the needs of the public schools for teachers especially trained for work in the kindergarten and lower primary grades. Manual training had been added in 1891.

The curriculum for 1900 shows the following outline of work. Four courses were required in general education: zoology, physics, manual training, and a choice in English taken from (1) forms of literature, (2) the study of a single period of English literature, (3) the intensive study of a single literary form, i.e. the drama, novel, epic, or lyric. These four courses constituted about 25 per cent of the two-year curriculum. In professional work, courses were prescribed in methods of teaching language, history, arithmetic, algebra and geometry, drawing, physical training, and music. Naturally some subject matter had to be considered as methods were discussed. Courses were also required in the history of education, science of education, psychology including development of the child, and practice teaching. All of this accounted for about 75 per cent of the total two-year course. It was an effective program for preparing teachers to go into the classroom with skills adequate to meet immediate problems, but it did not offer a broad, general education.

Besides the Trenton Normal School, city training schools existed in Newark, Bayonne, Jersey City, Paterson, Hoboken, Camden, and even in Trenton as the State school could not take all who applied from Mercer County. Agitation began for another institution to serve the northern part of the State, with the result that a second State normal school was opened in Upper Montclair in 1908. Then in 1913, the State took over the Newark City School and brought this under state control. Within a few years, a movement developed for a school in the southern part of the state, which resulted in the building of a school in Glassboro opened in 1923. In the same year the Legislature voted to take over the Paterson city school although no new building was erected. It was operated by the State for many years in the city building, which also contained an elementary school and was entirely inadequate in facilities for the education of teachers. A State school for Jersey City was then proposed; a site was acquired, and a building erected and opened in 1929. As the State expanded its service, the city training schools were closed so that teacher education became entirely a state function as far as public money was concerned. A few teachers came from private institutions but these were generally teachers above the elementary level.

Meanwhile, a decided step forward was taken by the Legislature in 1926 in placing the executive direction of the normal schools under the Commissioner of Education, subject to the approval of general policies by the State Board of Education. Previously each school had reported directly to the State Board, and the commissioner had no authority to integrate the teacher education program with the policies being recommended for general school work in the State. Although there were similarities, the curricula of the normal schools had differences and did not reflect a unified attack on the problem of teacher education. A two-year survey of teacher education from 1927 to 1929 brought forth many recommendations among which was the appointment of a Director of Teacher Education in 1928. Another extremely important change was the conversion of the school at Montclair from the preparation of elementary school teachers to that of high school teachers. Statistics in 1927 showed that over 85 per cent of the newly appointed high school teachers had gone outside the State for their preparation. This meant that in 1930 there were five State schools preparing elementary teachers, located in strategic areas of the State, and one preparing high school teachers.

Trenton, in 1917, had added curricula for teaching sub-normal and deaf children. The latter was carried out in cooperation with the New Jersey School for the Deaf. A three-year curriculum for music teachers, in both elementary and high schools, was added in 1919. Manual training had become a separate curriculum in 1915 and trained teachers for special work in that field in the middle and upper grades as well as in the high school. A special curriculum for rural education was also organized in 1917, but as rural schools became consolidated, this special work lasted only about a dozen years and then was absorbed back into the regular elementary curriculum.

In 1917, partly due to the low standards of physical fitness revealed among the entrants to the United States

Army in the First World War, the Legislature passed an act establishing physical training for all school pupils except kindergartners. The act required that two and a half hours a week be given to physical education and directed the State Board of Education to set up regulations for the qualifications of teachers and to require all students in the State normal schools to receive thorough instruction in these courses.

To meet the requirements of this law, the Trenton Normal School established a two-year program for teachers and supervisors of physical education. Thus, Trenton was not only educating teachers for the general program of the kindergarten and the elementary grades but also offering special curricula for teachers of the deaf, for rural teachers, and for teachers and supervisors of music, industrial arts, and physical education. Newark also had special curricula for fine and industrial arts in addition to the regular program. Paterson, Glassboro, and Jersey City offered only the regular curricula for kindergarten and the elementary grades. As the concepts of the schools broadened to include additional offerings to the pupils, the normal schools added these new fields to their curricula.

The Act of 1926, placing the normal schools under the supervision of the Commissioner of Education, produced immediate results in unifying the schools in a program designed to serve all the needs of the State, and in bringing about cooperation among the faculties toward their common ends. It gave teacher education new importance and added dignity. In that year, Trenton State Normal School was given the right to grant a bachelor's degree for the completion of a four-year program in its special curricula and for the teaching of general subjects in high school. Beginning with the class entering in 1929 a diploma in all of the schools for the elementary and special curricula required three years' work instead of two. The program for high school teachers organized at Montclair in 1928 was also of four years in length and led to a bachelor's degree. The extra year in the elementary curriculum was devoted entirely to additional courses of a general nature in the fields of the humanities, the sciences, and the social studies.

The new unification of the schools under the Commissioner of Education offered an opportunity for cooperative work by the faculties of the five schools involved in educating teachers for the elementary schools. New curricular patterns emerged putting more emphasis on general education. Nearly all of the additional year of the three-year program was devoted to general courses in the fields of English, science, and the social studies. The percentage of course-hours in professional work decreased although the total amount was about the same. Cooperation with the public schools in practice-teaching increased, which made the relationship profitable to both groups. The supervisors from the normal schools visited the public schools to check on the student teachers, and the teachers in the schools found out what the normal schools were doing by working with the student teachers.

In spite of the addition of the new schools to the State teacher education program, the supply of teachers with a two-year education did not keep up with the demand as the school population increased. In 1906, summer schools with free tuition were established by the State Board of Examiners operating independently of the normal schools. During the First World War the shortage became more acute, and high school graduates were given a temporary teaching certificate after attending one six-week summer session. This was renewed after attendance at succeeding summer sessions until at the end of six sessions, the teacher received a permanent certificate. Several hundred teachers came into the schools in this way until the free summer schools were finally abolished in 1932. Since that date tuition has been charged for summer school courses and their offerings have been geared to serve those who desired to secure credits for graduation from a teachers college, for certification requirements, or for graduate work.

Even with these teachers added to the normal school graduates, many teachers came to New Jersey from other states. In 1929-1930, for example, 34 per cent of the elementary teachers employed as of September came from outside the State.

Then a strange thing happened. With the economic depression beginning in 1930, a surplus of teachers developed. Teachers in the schools kept on teaching instead of resigning to be married or to enter other employment. Many of the normal school graduates could not secure positions after graduation. Economics affected the teaching profession as it does the market place. There, scarcity means higher prices and the stimulation of production; a surplus means lower prices and limitation of production. So in a service field like teaching, scarcity tends to increase salaries and to stimulate an increase in number of people preparing for the profession, whereas surplus tends to decrease wages or at least to hold them stationary and to limit the number preparing for the work.

One way to decrease the number of graduates was to increase the length of the course, thus producing fewer graduates with the same number of students in the school. For example, a school with six hundred students on a two-year program would graduate somewhat less than three hundred per year, whereas the same school of six hundred on a four-year basis would graduate somewhat less than one hundred fifty per year. Consequently the early thirties offered an opportunity to lengthen the curriculum again, strengthen the total program, and meet the condition of surplus which was not healthy for the graduates.

So serious was the financial condition of the State in the depression that an effort was made in the Legislature to close the schools in Newark and Paterson. Only determined efforts of the alumni and other interested citizens kept this from happening. Another step was to abolish free tuition, which had been in effect since 1855, and to charge $50 per year in 1932. This was increased to $100 in 1933, and again to $150 in 1956. With miscellaneous fees, the cost in 1963, exclusive of room and board and books, is about $240 per year.

The plan for a four-year curriculum leading to a bachelor's degree was approved by the State Board of Education and went into effect for the entering class of September, 1935, and all of the normal schools were renamed "Teachers Colleges." Following the pattern of earlier years, committees of the faculties working with the State office formulated new curriculum outlines and again put nearly all of the additional year into "general education." The curricula were not identical for the five schools but were fundamentally the same, giving nearly 70 per cent of the work to "general education" and about 30 per cent to "professional education" including practice teaching. Areas such as English, geography, history, music, art, and health and physical education were strengthened, and new courses in sociology and economics were added. The "general" courses were on a par with those of any good liberal arts college; the professional work was improved and brought up to date; and the added two years gave much more opportunity for the development of the personal and social fitness of the student. By 1940, therefore, eighty-five years after the establishment of the first normal school, New Jersey had arrived at a system of teacher education based on the principle that every teacher should hold a college degree obtained in a program which gave him a sound general education and proper professional preparation to have, at least, what one eminent educator called a "safety minimum" for beginning work in a classroom.

The colleges moved ahead on this new program, survived the strains of World War II, and arrived at the mid-century mark facing new challenges for improvement. The State Department of Education, therefore, initiated in 1953 a plan for a complete re-study of the curricula of the teachers colleges. This involved an advisory committee representing important lay groups, a commission from the State Department of Education, the colleges and the State University, and committees from the administrative and faculty groups in the colleges. A tremendous amount of study was carried on at each institution and many committe meetings were held with advice from the advisory groups. The result, adopted in 1956, established a new pattern based on the experiences of the previous years but presenting certain new features. Carefully thought-out objectives were prepared for the various elements of the curriculum and efforts were made to carry these objectives into the courses delineated.

The curriculum was divided into four sections: (1) general education to be taken by all, (2) courses related to the subject matter area in which the student specializes, (3) basic professional courses such as child development, and (4) professional courses in the area of specialization including practice teaching. Out of the 128 semester hours required, general education and courses in content fields were assigned from 65 per cent to 70 per cent of the total, and the professional education, including observation and student teaching, from 30 to 35 per cent. The courses in general education covered the major areas of the humanities, social studies, science, and mathematics. Certain choices were allowed and the different colleges could offer variations within the general pattern. Thus individuality within a State framework was permitted. It can be said, therefore, that after one hundred years of teacher education in the State, a point had been reached where the elementary teacher was recognized as needing the same quality of education as the high school teacher, and that this education aimed at producing a well-educated person in a general sense, fully cognizant of the subject matter to be taught, trained in the techniques of presenting this to young children, aware of psychological development, and experienced—to the limited degree permitted by time—through observation and student teaching. In practically the entire state, elementary teachers are on the same salary schedule as secondary teachers and differences between the salaries of women and men have been abolished. In many communities, additional amounts are granted for a fifth year of education. The Master's program for elementary teachers, begun at Trenton in 1947 with a small number of students, has spread to all of the colleges, with large enrollments in the extension program. In June, 1962, eighty Master of Arts degrees were awarded to those who had completed the required work in the elementary field.

According to a study made by the National Education Association for 1959-1960, New Jersey, with 25.1 per cent, ranked fifth among the 50 states in the percentage of elementary teachers with a master's degree. It also ranked fifth in salary paid to teachers for that year, with an average of $5871. This rose to $6308 in 1962-1963. Because of the decreased value of the dollar, however, this figure would be the equivalent of about one-half or $3154 in 1941, and one-third or $2100 in 1912.

How well have the teachers colleges succeeded in recruiting students who measure up to these advances? Much has been written to the effect that persons entering the teaching profession in this country do not rank as high intellectually as those in many other professions. There is plenty of evidence to the contrary in the case of teachers in New Jersey. Even in its early days, examinations for entrance to the Trenton State Normal School were given, thus establishing the right of the State to be selective, as opposed to the philosophy of many other states where any graduate of a high school may be admitted. In the early 1900's, each county had a quota six times the number of its representatives in the Legislature. This quota could be assigned to another county if not filled, but it assured a certain number of entrants from the rural counties. High school graduates were admitted on certificate, but those claiming the "equivalent" of a high school diploma had to take an examination.

After the first World War, there was criticism of candidates as deficient in arithmetic, spelling, and grammar, so the Board required tests in these fields from 1923 to 1929. Objection was made, however, that such examinations required review of work taken in the elementary school, so tests of subjects covered in the high school were substituted. Beginning in 1929 these tests were in English, American history, and general mathematics; a science test was added in 1937. Examinations were constructed by a faculty from the teachers colleges. In 1938, a speech test was added, and in 1941 definite weight was given to rank in class, to a personality rating from the high school, and to a personal interview at the college. A composite score was computed and the number of students admitted was decided in relation to the requirements of each curriculum for numbers of students who could be accommodated.

During the forties and fifties, standard tests compiled by testing bureaus and the Educational Testing Service were used. Typical of what usually occurs were the results of testing at Trenton Teachers College in 1947 when 495 took the examinations: 279 were certified for entrance, and 229 actually entered. For several years, Trenton gave the American Council Psychological Test to its freshmen in September. This test was composed of questions involving word meanings, reading comprehension, arithmetical computation, and items of general historical and scientific significance.

A comparison of the average raw scores made on this examination by freshmen at Trenton, for a ten-year period from 1935 to 1944, showed an average of 4.31 points above the record of four-year liberal arts college freshmen reported by the American Council.

The selective admission plan of the colleges resulted in an increasing number being admitted from the upper two quarters of high school classes. For example, at the Trenton college in 1934, 44.6 per cent came from the highest quarter, with 75.3 per cent from the upper half. In 1948, the percentage from the highest quarter was 56.4, with 88.3 per cent in the upper half. In 1959, of 3590 accepted in the six State colleges, 1931 or 54 per cent came from the upper quarter of their high school classes. These percentages offer a measure of the quality of students entering the teachers colleges.

Health and personality were also checked as the college realized that intellectual ability alone does not make a successful teacher. New Jersey's teacher education program since 1935, when it adopted the four-year curriculum for all students, has placed New Jersey among the leading states in selectivity of students and the efficiency of its preparation of these students for the work which they will face in the classroom.

Adaptation to the twentieth century demanded new sites, buildings, and equipment. In 1929, Trenton acquired about one hundred acres of wooded land at Hillwood Lakes, as the former site and facilities in the city had become entirely inadequate. Since the original purchase, another hundred acres has been added, and

Campus, Trenton State College, 1959, showing the buildings erected in the 1930's and those erected in the 1950's. The 200-acre campus provides ample space for the expansion of the 1960's and the future.

although progress was slow during the depression and both sites had to be used from 1931 to 1936, several buildings have been erected and more are under construction. The Newark Teachers College moved to a one hundred-acre site in Union near Elizabeth in 1958 and has built an entirely new plant. Glassboro has added eighty acres to its original fifty, has added several buildings and is erecting more. Paterson moved in 1951 to a site of about two hundred fifteen acres in Haledon and, like Newark, has built a new college. Jersey City has added a gymnasium, an arts and science building, and a food service building to its original plant.

Montclair has also greatly expanded its program for high schools and for special curricula, two of which, physical education and industrial arts, also serve the elementary schools.

To make possible all these improvements, the people of the State approved a bond issue of $15,000,000 in 1951 for the teachers colleges, and in 1959 approved another bond issue of $66,800,000 of which the six State colleges were assigned $29,950,000, the rest going to the State University and the Newark College of Engineering. This is in addition to about $10,000,000 spent from annual legislative appropriations to the different colleges from the acquisition of the Trenton site in 1929 to the bond issue in 1951. Buildings are going up on every campus in a frantic effort to keep up with the increasing demand for teachers which has resulted from the increasing population and school enrollment.

Additional buildings have made possible a very large increase in enrollment. From 2714 students in 1950, the six colleges have gone to 12,709 in 1962, with approximately 65 per cent preparing to teach in the elementary grades, or in special fields related to these grades. Yet it has been impossible to keep up with the demand for teachers. Elementary pupil enrollment in the State went from 664,189 in 1930 to 844,787 in 1962, now 73 per cent of the total enrollment. It is estimated that there will be a million pupils in the kindergartens and first to eighth grades in 1969, about 71 per cent of the total enrollment in the public schools of New Jersey.

The State Department of Education has plans to increase the enrollment in the six State colleges to 18,650 by 1965 and to 25,870 by 1970. This would mean a doubling of the present enrollment. To implement these plans, it will be necessary to secure funds for additional buildings in all of the colleges.

The need for teachers in the elementary schools has stimulated other colleges in the State to start or expand their facilities for educating teachers in this field. Besides Rutgers, the State University, five private colleges make distinct contributions, namely, Fairleigh Dickinson University, Seton Hall University, Caldwell College for Women, Georgian Court College, and Upsala College.

In 1962, the State Department of Education reported that of 5618 teachers appointed between October 30, 1960 and September 30, 1961 who had not taught during the previous year, only 1535 came from a New Jersey State college, 628 from other colleges in the State, and the rest from outside the state and various other sources. It was also necessary to employ 1021 from other states who had taught during the previous year. It is estimated that 115,000 teachers will be needed to replace those who leave the profession and to compensate for the growth of schools during the period from 1962 to 1975. Thus, the problem of securing a sufficient number of properly qualified teachers is still a major one just as it was one hundred years ago, although it should be recognized that the standards are much higher than they were then.

During the past fifty years it has been clear that the certification of teachers is parallel to the activities of the State in the education of teachers: in setting standards and in making it possible for many not attending the State colleges to enter into teaching. In 1911 the State Board of Examiners, which recommended to the State Board of Education rules for certification, consisted of the Commissioner of Education, the principals of the normal schools, a city superintendent, and a county superintendent. In 1936 a new Board was created, consisting of the Commissioner, one assistant commissioner, one president of a State teachers college, a county superintendent of schools, a city superintendent, a high school principal, a high school teacher, a principal of an elementary school, and an elementary teacher. Thus, a much wider representation of school work was achieved.

Under these Boards significant changes have been made and the rules have kept pace with rising standards and changing conditions. In 1924, examinations were abolished and course credits substituted. Some cities kept their separate certificates until 1930, when the State required all teachers to hold a State certificate. Certification requirement for elementary teachers were, for many years, not so high as graduation from the state teacher training institutions because of the shortage of teachers to fill positions. It has already been pointed out that in the 1920's, a person could begin teaching with only a high school diploma and one summer of professional work at a time when the normal school diploma required attendance of two years. The person who began teaching with this limited education had to take additional summer courses to keep the certificate valid. In the thirties, when the teachers college program went to four years, a State certificate could be secured with less preparation. It was not until 1948 that four years of college work were required for the limited elementary certificate.

The advance in requirements for the elementary certificate since the reorganization of the State Department of Education in 1911 may be summarized as follows:

1. In 1912—one year of high school
2. In 1913—two years of high school
3. In 1914—three years of high school
4. In 1915—high school diploma or equivalent
5. In 1916—high school and one session of pre-service summer school study in teacher preparation
6. In 1924—six summer school sessions to attain the permanent certificate

7. In 1928—one year of normal school followed by three summers of in-service training
8. In 1930—two years of normal school study
9. In 1932—three years of normal school study
10. In 1948—four years of professional and academic work in teachers college or equivalent

Constant advances have also been made in the certification of the school principal and supervisors. To be principal of a school with 12 teachers or more, the candidate must now have had three years of teaching experience, and a master's degree which must have included 24 credits in supervision and administration of education. Supervisors must have had similar education appropriate to their fields.

Unfortunately, however, since 1948 there have never been enough teachers to enforce the regulation completely and "provisional" and "emergency" certificates have had to be granted to fill vacancies, especially in rural and small town areas where lower salaries are paid. Requirements for these certificates have gradually been increased until, in 1963, a "provisional" certificate is granted to teachers from other states who have completed two years of normal school and have had two years of experience, or to those who have a Bachelor's degree and six credits in elementary education. The "emergency" certificate is granted to those who have 90 hours (three years) of college credits. It is expected that this will be raised in September, 1965, to a four-year degree from an accredited college or 90 hours of college work including at least 12 hours of work in the elementary field. Sub-standard certificates are renewable only if the applicant presents four semester hour credits of additional work, which thus provides for continuous study by the teacher.

The Bureau of Research of the State Deparment of Education reported in April 1962, that out of 48,756 teachers, there were some 6600 with substandard certificates. There was some improvement on the elementary level where the shift from emergency to provisional was marked. However, the figures showed that there was a shortage of 3880 teachers who could meet the standard requirements in the first through eighth grades, 383 in the kindergartens, and 372 in the classes for the mentally handicapped. Even with the greatly increased enrollments in the State colleges, it is doubtful if this shortage can be overcome in the near future, especially in view of the rapidly increasing pupil enrollments.

That such a situation is conducive to raising salaries in order to attract more persons into teaching is obvious. Elementary teachers in 1900 would have been astonished to know that in 1962 the average salary in the state would be $6308, with the lowest county average at $5657 and the highest at $6960, that elementary teachers would receive the same salary as secondary teachers, and that there would be no discrimination between men and women. Most graduates of the State colleges will be gettting from $4500 to $5000 per annum in their first year of teaching, and they can look forward to a maximum of from $7250 to $8500, after about thirteen years teaching. Indications are that these figures will be considerably higher in 1964. New Jersey now ranks among the highest five states in the country in salaries paid to teachers.

Why is New Jersey raising its standards and increasing its salaries? Perhaps one fundamental answer can be found in the address which the State Commissioner of Education, Dr. Frederick M. Raubinger, gave at the meeting of the New Jersey School Superintendents Association in Atlantic City on October 23, 1962, when he said:

> The School must be a good place for all. . . . The teacher must be able to inspire a student as well as to stuff knowledge into his head. . . . Good teaching is concerned with helping the pupil develop meaning and understanding. . . . Good teaching is concerned with influencing the behavior of pupils. . . . Good teaching is concerned with the student as a person and with his general development. . . . Good Teaching is the heart of the educational process.

Thus the leader of education in the State interprets all other phases of the school endeavor—buildings, books, equipment, administrators, specialists—as means to promote the major purpose of the entire education program: GOOD TEACHING.

The good teacher must have a clear understanding of the objectives of the school. The school's responsibilities are two-fold: partly to the society which supports it, and partly to the children who pass through its program. Society expects the school to inculcate in its children the ideals, past experiences, and present and future aspirations which determine the relationship of the children to society. For the good of both society and the children, they must be treated in such a way that their natures and individual possibilities will come to the greatest possible fruition within the framework of our democratic society.

The "Cardinal Principles" of 1918 can be re-worded to express the objectives of the present elementary school as follows: (1) to know the rules of good health and to follow practices to bring about physical fitness, (2) to have command of the fundamental processes of reading, writing, spelling, and arithmetic, (3) to have an intelligent understanding of the world in which we live in its historical, geographical, political, scientific, and cultural aspects, and (4) to possess moral qualities necessary for being a good citizen in our democracy. There is no fundamental opposition between the thorough acquisition of knowledge and the development of the creative talents of the individual. An increasing number of people are realizing that problems are not solved in a satisfactory manner unless people bring to bear on them the background of accurate knowledge pertinent to the problem under consideration. The elementary school must develop in its pupils a respect for the information which comes from study of the world of the past and of the marvelous age in which they live. More than ever before the school is the most important agency for preparing children to become active participants in a constantly changing society.

A visit to an elementary school will demonstrate how some of these ideals are being accomplished. The mathematics program, for example, has in recent years been completely revised so that today certain concepts formerly taught in the high school are presented in simple form in the elementary grades. Many youngsters of the middle elementary grades know more about science today than their parents did in the high school. Nuclear fission and space explorations are not strange concepts to them. Their knowledge of other countries has been greatly broadened by the new kinds of material introduced into their work in the social studies. Their accomplishments in art and music have improved markedly as increased opportunities for expression in these fields have been provided.

To provide for the continuous improvement in the efficiency of the elementary school there must also be an understanding of what every pupil can do, what he needs in order to enable him to reach his maximum of achievement, and how the techniques of the classroom can be adapted to adjust him to a changing world. Consequently, constant study of child growth and development must accompany the study of the materials to be taught and the techniques of teaching. America's dream of education for all children can be successful only if the people understand its fundamental objectives and appreciate what efforts must be made to provide the kind of educational establishment to bring about the realization of these objectives for all. It must be the aim of the *free, common, public* school to fulfill America's dream. To accomplish this ideal will take the determined support of every citizen.

BIBLIOGRAPHICAL NOTES

These notes give the titles of certain books useful as background for the entire period covered by this book. Particular books, dissertations, and reports of value as source material for each chapter are so listed. The date and place of publication of each book referred to are given only with the first reference in the notes for each chapter.

There are many books on the history of education in the United States. Among the most valuable is *Public Education in the United States* by Elwood P. Cubberly (Boston, 1919), which is a general history of education from colonial times to the second decade of the twentieth century. Attention is given to the battle for free schools, to the development of both elementary and high schools, and the new directions of the school in the first two decades of the twentieth century. Also useful for general material is *The Making of Our Middle Schools* by Elmer Ellsworth Brown (New York, 1903).

One of the most useful public documents is the *Report of the Commission to Survey Public Education* (Trenton, 1928), which is the report of the Joint Commission of the Legislature made by 15 educational experts. This report contains a brief history of education in the State, a discussion of the objectives of the different divisions of the school system, a description of the development of the various facilities offered by the educational system, and recommendations for improvement in practically all phases of the educational program.

Chapter I

For a history of the early settlement of New Jersey and progress until 1765 there is fascinating reading in *The History of the Colony of New Jersey* by Samuel Smith (Burlington,

1765; reprinted, Trenton, 1877). It contains the important documents connected with the surrender of the Dutch to the English in 1664, the division into East and West Jersey, the surrender by the Proprietors to the Queen in 1702, and the difficulties between the Assembly and the Governors following that date. It also reprints valuable memoranda between these two factions and thus gives a picture of the thinking of the leading men in the Colony.

For a more detailed account of the problems of education in the colonial period and particularly the contributions made by each religious sect, Nelson R. Burr's *Education of New Jersey, 1630-1871* (Princeton, 1942) contains very valuable material in a readable style. It describes the types of church schools, their contributions, and their difficulties. *The History of Education in New Jersey* by David Murray (Washington, 1899) also gives a description of early education in the state. It is less critical of school conditions than many other accounts. Anyone especially interested in the contributions of the Quakers will find a very comprehensive account in *Quaker Education in the Colony and State of New Jersey* by Thomas Woody (Philadelphia, 1923). Detailed descriptions are given of the actions of the Quarterly Meetings in Shrewsbury, Burlington, Salem, and Haddonfield. There is also a discussion of Quaker policy concerning education of the poor, apprenticeship, the curriculum, textbooks, and support. For those wishing to study further the work of different religious sects, the following are suggested: *A History of Religious Education in the Episcopal Church to 1835* by Clifton H. Brewer (New Haven, 1924); *American Presbyterianism, Its Origin and Early History* by Charles A. Briggs (New York, 1885), and *The Early Germans of New Jersey* by Theodore F. Chambers (Dover, 1904).

Chapter II

Both Burr's *Education* and Murray's *The History of Education in New Jersey* are full of valuable material concerning the development of education between the Revolutionary War and the adoption of the Constitution in 1844. Of special value in Murray's book are reminiscences by several people who attended school in the early decades of the nineteenth century.

For fascinating descriptions of school activities, discipline, and other such items in the 1820's, see three addresses by C. D. Deshler given to the New Brunswick Historical Society in 1892 (Rutgers University Library). For general background see *The American Common School* by Lawrence A. Cremin (New York, 1951). In interesting style this book gives an account of the roots of the common schools and discusses how it became an educational ideal. For those interested in legislative and financial developments, the *Annual State Reports* of the operations of the school systems of the State give an enormous amount of information with statistics. From 1839 to 1846 the Reports were made by the Trustees of the State School Fund. They are summaries of conditions, recommendations for change in distribution of the Fund and in legislative improvement, and contain statistics of school enrollment, costs, etc.

Chapter III

Again, much valuable material is contained in Burr's *Education in New Jersey,* in Murray's *The History of Education in New Jersey,* and in Cremin's *The American Common School.* The *Annual State Reports* make fascinating reading as, beginning in 1847, they contain not only a report by the State Superintendent of Schools but excerpts from the reports of the town superintendents. These men wrote with utter frankness concerning their difficulties, their dreams for the betterment of the schools, and what they thought should be done by the State authorities. After 1867, the reports of town superintendents do not appear, but there are detailed reports from the county superintendents. Reports of city superintendents begin in 1875 and continue until 1912. The report of 1879 is particularly valuable as it contains a 30-page history of the school system, written by Ellis Apgar, the State Superintendent of Schools. An examination of the American faith in education as related to changing political theory and our faith in democracy will be found in *Popular Education and Democratic Thought in America* by Rush Welter (New York, 1962). Two chapters deal with philosophy and practice in the colonial period. Roles played by labor, farm groups, and the middle class are also discussed. The story is brought down to the present time with a discussion of the progressive movement and of current trends in philosophical thinking as related to education.

Chapter IV

General discussion of the teacher problem can be found in the histories of education quoted in the general list. The books by Burr and Murray, previously cited, are also helpful. For a comprehensive discussion of this problem in New Jersey, see "The Professional Education of Teachers in New Jersey" by Edith Reed Shannon, a dissertation in the School of Education of New York University. This is a study of the professional education of teachers from the colonial period to 1932, with much correlative material concerning the relation of teacher competence and preparation to the development of the educational system. A more detailed account of the development of the teachers college at Trenton is found in "A History of the New Jersey State Teachers College at Trenton: 1855-1950" by Glenn E. Fromm, a dissertation in the School of Education of New York University. This describes in detail the development of the college with much material, also, concerning the campaign for teacher education in the first half of the nineteenth century. The history of the college is related to general educational advances. *Time the Great Teacher* by Rachel Jarrold and Glenn E. Fromm (Princeton, 1955) is a less formal account of the formation of the Trenton institution, its development and administration through its first hundred years. The book provides insights into student life and educational programs. Anyone interested in a day-by-day description of the material studied in the various courses of the normal school will find much of interest in the diary of Mary Jane (Sergeant) Larison in the Library of the Trenton State College. From October 1, 1855 to April 2, 1856, it records in detail what transpired in the classrooms, with full notes of work dictated by the instructors. The diary contains practically no items of personal life. In the *Reports of the State Department of Education,* previously referred to, there is a wealth of material from State officers and town superintendents, and later county superintendents, concerning their difficulties in securing good teachers and their interest in promoting more efficient teacher education.

Chapter V

For material concerning early textbooks, see the chapter in Murray's *History of Education in New Jersey* on this subject with accounts by George Plimpton, John Bodine Thompson, and C. D. Deshler. A very interesting description of the books used in the colonial period and of the development of new books after the Revolution is to be found in *Textbooks in Education* (New York, 1949). This work also discusses the use of books, how they were written, produced, and distributed. A vivid discussion of McGuffey's life and writing is found in *William Holmes McGuffey and His Readers* by Minnich (New York, 1936). Here will be found an account of his social beliefs, his competitors, his work as college president and professor, and much material concerning the relation of McGuffey's ideas to the frontier conditions in which he lived. The second volume of *Our Times* by Mark Sullivan (New York, 1927) has over two hundred pages devoted to the making of the American mind during the last quarter of the nineteenth century. Much attention is given to the influence of the schools on ideals, outlook, and general points of view. Many comments of famous people as to the influence the schools had on their thinking are cited. The *Annual State Reports,* especially from 1845 to 1900, reveal valuable details about what was being taught in the schools and which textbooks were being used. The annual catalogs and reports of the Trenton State Normal School from 1856 also contain much pertinent data concerning the elementary school course of study. "Trends in the Preparation of Teachers for the Elementary Schools at the New Jersey State Teachers College at Trenton," a dissertation by Evelyn B. Franz in the School of Education at Rutgers University, is a valuable study of the changing curricula for the preparation of teachers and of the requirements of the elementary school course of study.

Chapter VI

Among the many materials available for further reading on the ideas covered in this chapter, the author is indebted to Mark Sullivan's *Our Times,* already mentioned. All six volumes contain provocative material. A stimulating discussion of the beginnings of industrialization and of the unique contribution of Henry Ford can be found in *Image of America* by R. L. Bruckberger (New York, 1959). *The Transformation of the School* by Lawrence A. Cremin (New York, 1961) describes the traditions of popular education and the several philosophical and scientific movements which affected education during the nineteenth century and the efforts for reform appearing during the early years of the twentieth century. It discusses the rise of so-called progressive education, the changes in the original doctrines made by disciples of Dewey, and the demise of the official movement. It has outstanding reference to general social thinking. Among the many books concerning the present-day elementary school, a recent publication, *Teaching and Learning in the Elementary School* by Dorothy Petersen and Velma Hayden (New York, 1961), is one of the best comprehensive presentations of the curriculum as it exists today. It traces the emergence of the curriculum from early concepts, its development, and gives contradictory phases of theories of method with detailed discussions of the objectives and content of each subject. It also presents suggestions for accommodating individual differences and adapting the school to the changing ideas of the present world. For comparative statistics, the *Research Bulletins* of the National Education Association are of inestimable value. *Economic Status of Teachers in 1961-1962* contains much pertinent data. *The Tenth Report of the Commission on State Tax Policy* (Trenton, 1963) is a thorough presentation of the present taxation situation in the State, with data on current tax scales and distribution and comparisons with taxes in other states. The goals, costs, and taxes for schools are discussed with a complete review of state aid for local districts and recommendation of changes. Reports from the office of the Commissioner of Education are also very helpful in studying the subjects covered by this chapter.

Chapter VII

The catalogs of the Trenton Normal School (later Teachers College, now State College) are of special usefulness, because the Annual Report of the President is contained in each catalog with a discussion of developments. Catalogs of the State schools at Montclair, Newark, Glassboro, Paterson, and Jersey City are also helpful. The annual reports of the State Superintendent of Schools also contain pertinent information. From 1911 on, the reports are made by the Commissioner of Education and his assistants. The *Reports of the Bureau of Research* of the State Department of Education provide data on enrollment, teacher need and supply, and school building progress. The Report of the Survey in 1928, mentioned before, is also valuable. Developments in teacher certification from 1848 to 1954 are comprehensively described in "State Certification of Teachers in New Jersey" by Olive H. Todd, a dissertation in the School of Education of Rutgers University. This study details all the changes that have been made and their relationship to the administration of schools, teachers' salaries, and other factors. An excellent general discussion of the relationship of good teaching to our society is contained in *Teachers for Our Times* (Washington, 1944), which was the initial volume published by the Commission on Teacher Education of the American Council on Education.

INDEX

THE NEW JERSEY HISTORICAL SERIES

Published Under the Auspices of

STATE OF NEW JERSEY TERCENTENARY COMMISSION

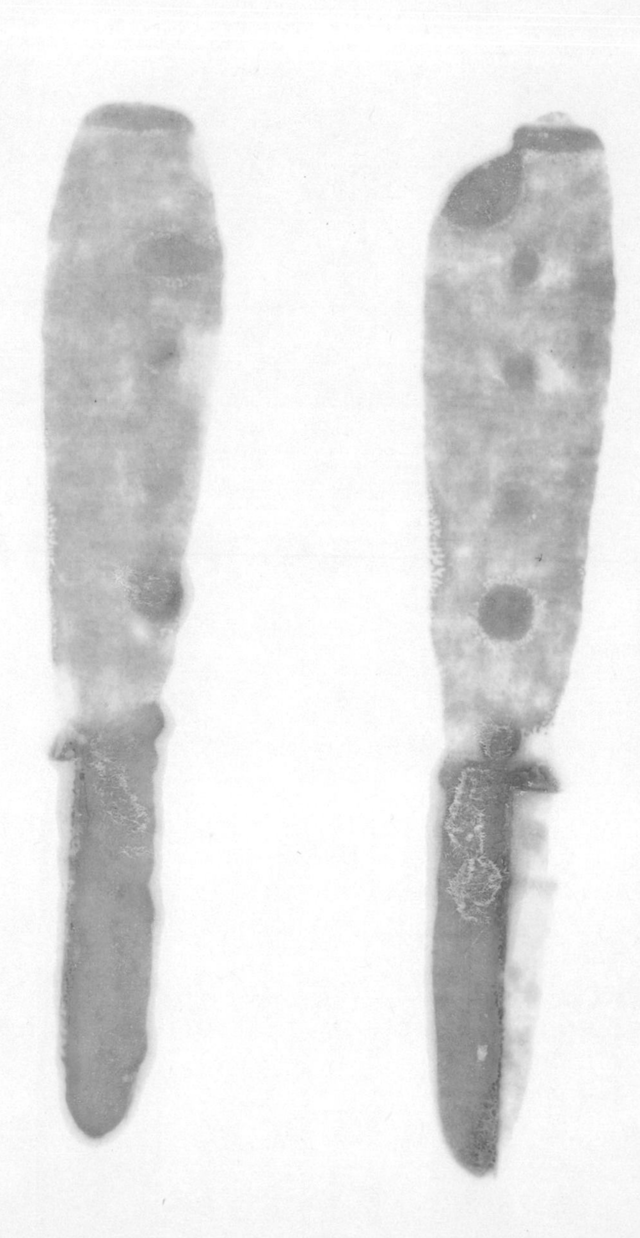

NEW JERSEY TODAY

With selected historic sites

State Capital
County Seats
County Boundaries
Toll Highways
Other Important Highways
Interstate Route Numbers (80)
Federal Route Numbers (22)
State Route Numbers (70)
Selected Railroads
Abandoned Canals

SCALE OF MILES
0 10 20 30 40 50

NEW YORK
SUSSEX
PASSAIC
BERGEN
WARREN
MORRIS
ESSEX
HUDSON
UNION
HUNTERDON
SOMERSET
MIDDLESEX
MERCER
MONMOUTH
KITTATINNY MTS.

High Point 1,803
Montague
Sussex
Greenwood Lake
Hamburg
Branchville
Wallkill R.
Franklin
Ringwood
Mahwah
Hackensack R.
Wallpack Bend
Tocks I.
Paulins Kill
Newton
Ogdensburg
Lake Mohawk
Sparta
Newfoundland
Wanaque Res.
Oakland
Butler
Wyckoff
Ridgewood
Oradell Res.
Erie-Lackawanna
Blairstown
Lake Hopatcong
Pompton Lakes
Hawthorne
Bergenfield
Delaware Water Gap
Picatinny Arsenal
Paterson
Teaneck
Englewood
Columbia
Hope
Wharton
Boonton
Hackensack
Netcong
Denville
Clifton
Garfield
Ft. Lee
Delaware
Budd Lake
Dover
Succasunna
Parsippany
Caldwell
Passaic
Hackettstown
Montclair
Bloomfield
Belvidere
Morristown
Livingston
W. Orange
E. Orange
Weehawken
Union City
Hoboken
Jersey City
Long Valley
Mendham
Madison
Maplewood
Newark
Turnpike
Washington
Morris Canal
Hampton
Phillipsburg
Musconetcong
Spruce Run Res.
Bernardsville
Summit
Irvington
Union
High Bridge
Berkeley Hts.
Elizabeth
Bayonne
Alpha
Central R.R. of N.J.
Round Valley Res.
Plainfield
Westfield
Linden
Rahway
Clinton
Carteret
Milford
Somerville
S. Plainfield
Garden State Parkway
New Jersey Turnpike
Raritan
Bound Brook
Metuchen
Woodbridge
Frenchtown
Manville
Edison
Raritan R.
Flemington
New Brunswick
South Amboy
Perth Amboy
Raritan Bay
Fort Hancock
Sandy Hook
Sergeantsville
Sayreville
Keansburg
South River
Keyport
Atlantic Highlands
Stockton
Raven Rock
Hopewell
Reading Railway
Raritan Canal
Matawan
Middletown
Spotswood
Rumson
Lambertville
Princeton
Pennsylvania R.R.
Red Bank
Fort Monmouth
Englishtown
New Shrewsbury
Long Branch
Lawrenceville
Plainsboro
Delaware & Raritan Canal
Railroad
Eatontown
Washington Crossing
Freehold
Hightstown
West Trenton
Trenton
Asbury Park
Neptune